Mark Robinson

E-LEARNING IN AVIATION

This book is dedicated to Mike, Katie, Sam and Andy

e-Learning in Aviation

SUZANNE K. KEARNS
University of Western Ontario, Canada

ASHGATE

© Suzanne K. Kearns 2010

All rights reserved. No part of this publication may be reproduced, stored in a retrieval system or transmitted in any form or by any means, electronic, mechanical, photocopying, recording or otherwise without the prior permission of the publisher.

Suzanne K. Kearns has asserted her right under the Copyright, Designs and Patents Act, 1988, to be identified as the author of this work.

Published by
Ashgate Publishing Limited
Wey Court East
Union Road
Farnham
Surrey, GU9 7PT
England

Ashgate Publishing Company
Suite 420
101 Cherry Street
Burlington
VT 05401-4405
USA

www.ashgate.com

British Library Cataloguing in Publication Data
Kearns, Suzanne K.
  e-Learning in aviation. -- (Ashgate studies in human
  factors for flight operations)
  1. Aeronautics--Safety measures--Computer-assisted instruction.
  2. Airplanes--Piloting--Safety measures--Computer-assisted instruction.
  3. Aeronautics--Safety measures--Study and teaching.
  4. Airplanes--Piloting--Safety measures--Study and teaching.
  5. Instructional systems--Design.
  I. Title II. Series
  629.1'3252'0785-dc22

  ISBN: 978-0-7546-7879-3 (hbk)
        978-0-7546-9734-3 (ebk)

Library of Congress Cataloging-in-Publication Data
Kearns, Suzanne K.
  E-learning in aviation / by Suzanne K. Kearns.
      p. cm.
  Includes bibliographical references and index.
  ISBN 978-0-7546-7879-3 (hardback) -- ISBN 978-0-7546-9734-3 (ebook)
  1. Aeronautics--Study and teaching. 2. Computer-assisted instruction. 3. Web-based instruction. I. Title.
  TL560.K43 2010
  629.1078'5--dc22
                                                                2010017057

Printed and bound in Great Britain by
MPG Books Group, UK

Contents

List of Figures   *vii*
List of Tables   *ix*
List of Abbreviations   *xi*
Reviews for e-Learning in Aviation   *xiii*

PART I	THE EFFECTIVENESS, THEORY, AND APPLICATION OF E-LEARNING IN AVIATION	
1	The Life of Aviation Training	3
2	What is e-Learning?	11
3	Does e-Learning Work?	23
4	Foundational e-Learning Theories	31
5	The Feasibility of e-Learning for Nontechnical Skills	43
6	Incorporating Practice into e-Learning	55
PART II	INSTRUCTIONAL DESIGN FOR E-LEARNING IN AVIATION	
7	Instructional Design for e-Learning	69
8	Analysis	75
9	Design	107
10	Development	131
11	Implementation	145
12	Evaluation	153

References   *167*
Index   *177*

List of Figures

Figure 7.1	The ADDIE model of instructional design	70
Figure 9.1	A blended learning strategy for aviation training	115
Figure 9.2	Overview of the instructional hierarchy	121
Figure 9.3	The organization of modules	123
Figure 9.4	Storyboard	128
Figure 11.1	The e-learning implementation process	146
Figure 12.1	A reaction survey for e-learning	159
Figure 12.2	Return on investment formula	163
Figure 12.3	Return on investment for e-learning in TransAsia Airways	164

List of Tables

Table 8.1	Task analysis decision matrix	95
Table 9.1	Synchronous vs. asynchronous e-learning	112
Table 9.2	Analysis of training objectives for blended learning	114
Table 9.3	Examples of training activities	124
Table 10.1	File size limit associated with Internet connection speed	140

List of Abbreviations

ADDIE	Analyze, design, develop, implement, evaluate
AICC	Aviation industry computer-based training committee
AMT	Aircraft maintenance technician
ATC	Air traffic control
CBI	Computer-based instruction
CBL	Computer-based learning
CBT	Computer-based training
CLT	Cognitive load theory
CMC	Computer-mediated communication
CRM	Crew resource management
CTA	Cognitive task analysis
DE	Distance education
EICAS	Engine indicating and crew alerting system
e-Learning	Electronic learning
EPSS	Electronic performance support systems
ETA	Estimated time enroute
F2F	Face-to-face
FAA	Federal aviation administration
FBO	Fixed-base operator
FOQA	Flight operations quality assurance
GA	General aviation
GMP	Guided mental practice
ID	Instructional design
IMC	Instrument meteorological conditions
IPT	Instrument procedure trainer
IRR	Inter-rater reliability
ISD	Instructional system design
IT	Information technology
JAA	Joint aviation authority
LMS	Learning management system
LOFT	Line oriented flight training
LOMS	Line operations monitoring system
LTM	Long-term memory
M-learning	Mobile learning
PBL	Problem-based learning
PC	Personal computer
PDA	Personal digital assistant
RFP	Request for proposal

ROI	Return on investment
SBT	Scenario-based training
SCORM	Shareable content object reference model
SME	Subject matter expert
SMS	Short message service
SOP	Standard operating procedure
SOW	Statement of work
SRM	Single-pilot resource management
T-3	Train the trainer
TCAS	Traffic collision avoidance system
TOT	Transfer of training
USD	United States dollars
VFR	Visual flight rules
VLJ	Very-light jet
WBT	Web-based training
WM	Working memory
WMD	Wireless mobile devices

Reviews for e-Learning in Aviation

'*e-Learning in Aviation* provides an excellent comprehensive introduction to the most salient topics that should be considered in the application of effective learning strategies, teaching methodologies, and information technologies for aviation training in today's rapidly changing global and digital environments. Various models of experiential learning, that integrate the latest e-Learning innovations with the social or human factors context, are an important feature that will undoubtedly enhance the students' learning outcomes. This book will also appeal to those managers who are considering new learning management platforms to develop a more productive and effective aviation organization. It is most essential and highly recommended.'

K. Victor Ujimoto, University of Guelph, Canada

'At a time when aviation is turning attention to the needs of the next generation of aviation professionals, and when international standards are opening pathways to competency-based training, this book is an important addition to the literature. In the years ahead, the demand for aviation professionals will exceed supply. Training capacity will be stretched to the limit. Learning methodologies will have to respond to the learning styles of a new generation. Suzanne Kearns helps us see how learning in aviation can respond to to the changes that are taking place and how we can use new thinking and new tools to make our training more effective and more efficient. All of this will help us bring more knowledgeable and more skilled—more competent—employees to the aviation workplace. The dividends of competency will be paid out in improved safety results and more efficient flight operations.'

Jim Dow, Chief, Flight Training and Examinations, Government of Canada

'Suzanne Kearns addresses the issues facing those of us actively engaged in aviation education and training in a balanced and well thought out manner. She raises points that are at the heart, encouraging deep learning which should be the goal of all aviation education and training organisations. This book is essential reading for anyone who is serious about "good teaching" in the aviation environment.'

Paul Bates, Griffith University, Australia

'*e-Learning in Aviation* leads us on a journey from the early days of apprenticeship and simulation to the sophisticated world of performance-based training techniques. The book is more than just a review of the various shapes and forms of e-Learning. It aids decision makers determine their training strategies, and it sets out the processes that practitioners should follow in order to implement eLearning from scratch. Suzanne Kearns writes in an engaging style, and does not shy from addressing the pros as well as the cons of e-Learning in equal measure. She highlights the key theories about how we all learn, drawing intelligently from the vast array of literature on the subject. It is indeed refreshing to find an e-Learning book that is genuinely aimed at aviation, and in so doing the author has gifted the industry with a blueprint that has the potential to bring about real change in the effectiveness of training.'

Paul Clark, Managing Director, Through The Looking Glass

Ashgate Studies in Human Factors for Flight Operations

Series Editors

R. Key Dismukes, Ph.D.
Chief Scientist for Human Factors at the NASA Ames Research Center, California, USA

Capt. Daniel E. Maurino
Coordinator of the Flight Safety and Human Factors Study Programme at the International Civil Aviation Organization (ICAO), Quebec, Canada

Sidney Dekker, Ph.D.
Professor of Human Factors and Flight Safety, and Director of Research at the School of Aviation, Lund University, Sweden

Ashgate Studies in Human Factors for Flight Operations is a series dedicated to publishing high-quality monographs and edited volumes which contribute to the objective of improving the safe and efficient operation of aircraft.

The series will achieve this by disseminating new theoretical and empirical research from specialists in all relevant fields of aviation human factors. Its foundation will be in applied psychology, presenting new developments and applications in such established fields as CRM, SA and decision-making. It will also encompass many other crucial areas such as fatigue and stress, the social environment, SMS, design, technology, communication and training.

Submitted work relevant to the objective of the series will be considered for publication by the board of editors. The series is intended for an international readership and so books with a broad geographical appeal are especially encouraged.

PART I
The Effectiveness, Theory, and Application of e-Learning in Aviation

Chapter 1
The Life of Aviation Training

Life is a culmination of the past, an awareness of the present, an indication of a future beyond knowledge, the quality that gives a touch of divinity to matter.

—Charles Lindbergh

Overview

The purpose of this chapter is to familiarize the reader with:

- the four generations of aviation training: apprenticeship, simulation, safety, and customized training;
- how our current method of training effectively sorts the good from the bad, but does not maximize the skills, abilities, and attitudes of the good;
- why e-learning is a tool that challenges the paradigm of aviation training;
- the advantages and disadvantages of e-learning;
- the importance of thorough instructional design in the e-learning development process.

Introduction

The purpose of this book is to examine the use of e-learning in aviation, as e-learning is part of the industry's future. However, before we look forward we must first consider the past. The life of aviation training can be broadly segregated into four generations: apprenticeship, simulation, safety, and customized training. It is important to note that each subsequent generation of training enriches, rather than replaces, the previous ones.

First Generation: Apprenticeship (1903–1929)

Traditionally, since the Wright brothers accomplished the first powered and controlled flight on December 17, 1903, and began to teach others the art of powered heavier-than-air flight, they established the foundation of aviation training, which still remains in modern-day pilot training. The basic structure of this training includes classroom training, more commonly referred to as ground school, and in-aircraft training conducted according to an apprenticeship model. Through apprenticeship, experienced pilots guide novice pilots by means of skill demonstrations and knowledge transmission, until student skills attain a level of competency. The goal of instruction is for pilots to perform maneuvers within specifications (such as ± 100 feet or ± 10 degrees).

Second Generation: Simulation (1929–1979)

The Link trainer was invented in 1929; it soon became widely available, and the next generation of aviation training was born. With the introduction of flight simulation, flight schools were no longer dependent on weather conditions to conduct flight training. Originally developed for instrument and systems training, simulators have evolved to the point where they incorporate high-fidelity visual displays and can now be used for all aspects of flight training. Having been trained in modern flight simulators, the first time a pilot conducts a flight in a large commercial aircraft, he or she will probably be carrying a load of passengers. In the second generation, training was still conducted under an apprenticeship model with classroom and in-aircraft training (supplemented by simulator training), and the objective of training was still the mastery of flight performance standards. After the introduction of simulation, much of the focus of the aviation industry was on improving aircraft systems and components, including early airworthiness certification and pilot licensing, air-cooled engines, and slotted wings in the 1940s and early 1950s; the introduction of jet engines, radar, and precision approaches in the late 1950s and early 1960s; and ground and traffic collision avoidance devices in the early 1970s. However, the next generation of aviation training did not begin until 1979.

Third Generation: Safety (1979–Present)

The third generation of aviation training began with a NASA conference in 1979, at which representatives from several major airlines met to discuss the alarming number of human-error-caused accidents in the aviation industry. The result of this conference was Crew Resource Management (CRM) training, which entails 'the effective use of all resources (hardware, software and liveware) to achieve safe and efficient flight operations' (Jensen 1995: 116). CRM training was revolutionary at the time, as it was dramatically different from traditional ground instruction that focused exclusively on air knowledge (including weather, air law, meteorology, and aircraft systems). In fact, CRM training was so different that there was some backlash from pilots who viewed it as 'psycho-babble' (Helmreich, Merritt and Wilhelm 1999). However, attitudes have changed, and annual CRM training is now mandatory for most airline and military pilots. Training is still conducted under an apprentice model, with ground school, and simulator or in-aircraft training. However, elements of CRM safety training have been implemented into each of these aspects of training. This generation of aviation training reflects the current state of the industry.

Fourth Generation: Customized Training

Our current training paradigm was not designed for learning; it was designed for sorting learners (Reigeluth 1994). Consider for a moment how students are typically evaluated, then sorted into letter grades (A, B, C) or pass–fail. When instruction is standardized, it provides companies with a valid and simple method of comparing students with one another. According to Reigeluth (1999: 18), standardized instruction was an important need in the industrial age: separating the laborers from the managers. After all, you couldn't afford to—and didn't want to—educate the common laborers too much, or they wouldn't be content to do boring, repetitive tasks, nor to do what they were told to do without questions.

Perhaps this perspective reflected the early generations of aviation training. Instruction was more focused on following procedures than on decision-making or problem-solving skills. However, the training needs of the industry have advanced. The increasing congestion of airspace, advanced technology in the cockpit, and an influx of low-time pilots into the airline sector present unique training challenges. To produce better pilots more rapidly, the industry cannot provide less training but must fundamentally rethink the way training is delivered and must ultimately train more efficiently.

It has become evident that a mastery of standard operating procedures (SOPs) is insufficient preparation for every possible situation, as anomalies arise and pilots must possess the critical thinking skills necessary to solve complex and novel problems. Therefore, training pilots as you would assembly-line workers (first you do A, then do B, C, and D) is inadequate. Pilot training must shift from a sorting method (adequate vs. inadequate) toward a learning method (maximizing the performance of each individual).

The way to make this happen is by giving each and every learner the time and training needed to reach their maximum level of performance. This approach represents a fundamental shift in aviation training; it focuses on customization, not standardization (Reigeluth 1999).

An additional drawback of older methods is that training is based on conformity and compliance. Learners are expected to sit down, be quiet, and do what the instructor says. Ironically, within this contextual environment, we try to teach pilots how to take the initiative and think critically. Therefore, changing the content of the training material is not sufficient, because 'the very structure of our systems of training and education discourages initiative and diversity' (Reigeluth 1999).

The training paradigm itself needs to be changed!

Having training performance standards is extremely important—but should these standards be regarded as the maximum level of performance, or the minimum? It can be argued that performance standards are a method of sorting, of separating acceptable performance from the unacceptable. What this pass–fail style of training does not do is maximize the performance of individuals at the top end of the spectrum. Is this truly the best way to train? Or should learners continue with training until they each attain their unique maximum performance level? This way, the performance standard would be considered the *minimum* acceptable level of performance. Although each pilot would achieve a different level of performance, all pilots would be above the minimum.

This need for change is evident in the industry, as aviation is at the threshold of a revolutionary new approach to pilot training: performance-based training. Performance-based training is built upon the foundation of the previous three generations of training, with one radical difference. Rather than providing student pilots with a predetermined number of practice hours on certain maneuvers or phases of flight training, as mandated by current regulations, performance-based training allows training to be tailored to the skill of each student. Students receive practice on skills they are weakest in and do not waste time on areas they have already mastered. Regulators worldwide are opening regulatory doors for this approach, allowing high-quality flight training institutions an alternate means of complying with pilot licensing requirements.

Performance-based training provides a tremendous opportunity for aviation trainers to rethink the methods by which training is delivered. Consider the question: Should we train pilots with the most effective methodologies or with traditional methodologies (because that is the way it has always been done)? There is a tremendous opportunity for e-learning within performance-based licensing structures. e-Learning that incorporates adaptive instruction and practice can continually challenge and improve the skills of each individual pilot until further practice fails to produce additional performance improvements. This philosophy of training focuses on making each individual pilot the best he or she can be, not simply on sorting those with the 'right stuff' from those who just don't make the cut. This option would require a continual training cycle, rather than an annual one. With current training methods, a continual training cycle would be prohibitively expensive. However, with electronic learning (e-learning) it is a feasible option.

The Advantages and Disadvantages of e-Learning

e-Learning has several advantages over classroom instruction, including:

- cost-efficiency;
- geographic flexibility, as the course can be taken in any location;
- temporal flexibility, as training is available 24/7;
- content standardization between instructors across an entire organization;
- interactive exercises;
- compatibility; software has now become standardized, so practically any computer can run training in an identical fashion;
- immediate learner feedback, tailored specifically to exhibited performance;
- automatic tracking of learner performance within a company-wide database.

However, an important point to consider is that none of these advantages will come to fruition if the e-learning is not built upon sound instructional design principles, and specifically tailored to the needs of the student and the organization. There is a very wide range in quality of e-learning programs. In fact, when researchers review the effectiveness of e-learning compared to classroom instruction, they find that some computer-based courses significantly outperform their classroom-based counterparts. However, an equally large percentage of e-learning courses significantly underperform classroom-based training (Bernard et al. 2004). These findings illustrate the point that not all e-learning is effective. There are also several disadvantages associated with e-learning, including the following:

- course design, creation, and implementation can cost more than the projected savings;
- training success is dependent on the learner's ability to use computers;
- learners require a higher level of motivation and self-direction;
- it is difficult for instructors to ensure that learners are paying attention;
- the learners and the organization must be prepared to accept e-learning;
- learners lose direct contact with their instructor in asynchronous learning environments, or nonverbal cues such as body language and voice inflection in synchronous learning environments (see Chapter 2);
- it is not as simple as delivering a traditional classroom-based course over the Internet; the entire premise must be rethought (Piskurich 2006).

Ironically, an e-learning course that has been created to save money on training costs can end up being very expensive once you factor in course development and the possibility of training inefficiency. Unfortunately, poorly designed e-learning solutions are quite common. Companies that are eager to save training costs jump on the e-learning bandwagon without fully understanding how to make this type of training effective. The most common approach is to simply take a classroom-based course and create an identical computer-based version, expecting good learning outcomes. The products used to convert classroom-based courses into e-learning often promise clients a course that is ready to implement in just a few weeks. This type of software merely converts PowerPoint slides into a web-based training (WBT) program. The best outcome in this situation is that students will finish the course with the same level of knowledge and skill as was previously produced in a classroom-based course. However, it is far more likely that students will learn less, because the learning materials were not designed with computer-based delivery in mind. In addition, it only takes exposure to one poorly designed training program for a group of learners to boycott e-learning altogether.

Just as flight simulation did not replace in-aircraft training, e-learning should not necessarily replace traditional classroom instruction. e-Learning does not eliminate the need for well-qualified human instructors; instead, it should capitalize on the expertise of instructors and provide them with the technology to rethink how they train. Technology will never be able to teach; good teaching will always depend on effective instructors.

e-Learning revolutionizes how instructors interact with students. In a classroom setting, it is common for a small handful of students to answer all of the instructor's questions. Unfortunately, the instructor has no way of determining if the others in the class are keeping up with the material or are hopelessly lost, until they encounter a quiz or a final exam. The interactivity of e-learning allows instructors to assess and track performance more frequently, and to intervene when a student is falling behind.

e-Learning should not be viewed as a complete replacement of classroom instruction, but simply another tool that an organization and an instructor possess to maximize the efficiency of learning. When implemented appropriately, e-learning does not reinvent the wheel, but redesigns it. Although e-learning has its place in the third generation of aviation training, it is anticipated that with the shift to customized training methods, its use will become a part of every pilot's training program.

Conclusion

The purpose of this book is to assess the strengths and weaknesses of various methods of e-learning, describe appropriate instructional design strategies, and detail practical guidelines for the development of effective e-learning. This work will serve as a resource for aviation training professionals and will help to bring e-learning instructional design theory to practice. Hopefully, using the knowledge contained in this book, aviation trainers will no longer be bystanders in e-learning instructional design, but will be able to actively participate in the analysis, design, development, and evaluation of e-learning programs. Not only should this involvement result in more efficient courses, but it will save aviation organizations money because they will not have to hire e-learning developers to complete their instructional design.

Practical Summary

- The life of aviation training can be broken down into four broad categories, each building upon, rather than replacing, the previous generations:
    - apprenticeship, which focuses on modeling an instructor until knowledge, skills, and attitudes are passed down;
    - simulation, which integrates synthetic flight environments for practice;
    - safety, which adds human factors training to the pilot curriculum;
    - customized training, which represents the future of aviation training; it focuses on maximizing the skills and abilities of each individual pilot

in the most efficient manner (without wasting time practicing skills that have already been mastered).
- e-Learning is a tool that will likely be used increasingly under the paradigm of customized training.
- There are several advantages and disadvantages associated with e-learning:
  - however, the best way to maximize the strengths of e-learning is through careful instructional design and an understanding of which attributes have been shown to improve learning, and which are probably ineffective.

Chapter 2
What is e-Learning?

> I think it's fair to say that personal computers have become the most empowering tool we've ever created.
>
> They're tools of communication, they're tools of creativity, and they can be shaped by their user.
>
> —Bill Gates

Overview

The purpose of this chapter is to review the definition of e-learning, delivery methods, technology, and characteristics of modern e-learning, specifically:

- the history of e-learning, including some problems of early computer-based training;
- how the Internet has revolutionized e-learning;
- e-learning delivery methods, including synchronous, asynchronous, and blended learning;
- technology of modern e-learning, including:
  - mobile learning
  - learning management systems
  - rapid repurposing.
- characteristics of modern e-learning, including:
  - self-pacing
  - adaptive e-learning
  - collaboration and learning communities
  - e-learning for nontechnical pilot training.

A Brief History of e-Learning

Rosenberg (2001) explains that e-learning did not begin with computer-based training. Rather, in the early 1920s Thomas Edison predicted that motion pictures would replace textbooks. Obviously, this prediction did not come true, but it did lead to the first type of e-learning, the military training film. The military was one of the first organizations with a workforce distributed throughout the world, and there were concerns that the thoroughness and consistency of training would be lost overseas. Training videos were therefore a welcome and effective method of delivering information.

It wasn't until the late 1980s that a new electronic method of delivering training became available: personal computers, which made computer-based training (CBT) feasible. CBT typically consisted of software that was installed on a specific computer's hard drive or delivered via CD-ROM. Aircraft manufacturers began supplying CBT to their customers at this time. However, airlines had to spend enormous amounts of money on the hardware and software required to run each manufacturer's proprietary CBT. For this reason, the Aviation Industry CBT Committee (AICC) was created in 1988 as an international association of training professionals who develop CBT guidelines for the aviation industry. The first objective of the AICC was to standardize hardware requirements and promote interoperability (Costello 2002).

In general, early CBT had four major issues working against it:

1. There were so many platforms in use that it was impossible for the training technology to keep up.
2. Hardware and software limitations made training boring, as it was based mostly on long readings followed by a few short questions.
3. Content instability and high development costs made organizations reluctant to invest money into e-learning.
4. Lack of understanding of e-learning instructional design concepts diminished the effectiveness of training (Rosenberg 2001).

Overall, e-learning was not living up to its expectations. So, what changed? The innovation that revolutionized e-learning is the Internet. Modern e-learning is characterized by training that is accessed via an Internet or intranet connection. In this manner, training programs are accessible via any computer on an on-demand basis.

Think for a moment beyond the scope of organization-based training. The Internet has revolutionized how an entire generation of people access information. An almost limitless number of learning resources are accessible online, including novels, textbooks, academic journal articles, newspapers, and free educational resources such as wikis, including Wikipedia (www.wikipedia.org) and Skybrary (www.skybrary.aero). The Internet has fundamentally changed how the next generation of aviation professionals access information, as they will likely be more comfortable referencing electronic resources than paper-based ones.

e-Learning is now widely utilized; in 2003 it was reported that 95 percent of survey respondents utilized some e-learning in their organizations (Derouin, Fritzsche and Salas 2005). After analyzing a survey they had distributed to business pilots, Raisinghani and colleagues (2005) determined that pilots are comfortable with new technology and capable of utilizing e-learning. Overall, they concluded that e-learning, rather than traditional face-to-face instruction, supports the training requirements of modern pilots.

Definition of e-Learning

What is e-learning? *e-Learning* is a shortened version of the term *electronic learning*. This method of training provides educational materials, computer-mediated communication (CMC), and the delivery of instructional content through electronic technology (Eddy and Tannenbaum 2003). This electronic technology may take the form of the Internet or an organization's intranet. Researchers and anyone involved in education typically compares e-learning against instruction that is conducted in a classroom setting. Several different terms are used to refer to classroom-based learning, including face-to-face (F2F), traditional classroom, or brick-and-mortar instruction.

Distance education (DE) is the broadest term used in the literature, and includes all training that is provided to learners who are not physically present in a classroom with an instructor. However, DE includes a variety of delivery mediums ranging in sophistication from web-based instruction enhanced with videos and simulations, to a textbook with paper-and-pencil quizzes completed through correspondence. e-Learning is a refinement of DE, including only courses that are conducted via distance and that utilize an electronic instructional medium.

e-Learning Delivery Methods

e-Learning is broken down into three broad categories: synchronous, asynchronous, and blended learning.

Synchronous

Synchronous e-learning takes place when learners and an instructor log in to a virtual classroom simultaneously at a predetermined time from their separate locations. This method of e-learning is community based and typically incorporates some form of live CMC using either a webcam and headset with a microphone, or instant messaging software.

Asynchronous

Asynchronous e-learning, by comparison, is completed independently by each learner. Although CMC may be used, it is in the form of an electronic mailing list or message board in which learners post comments to a forum for classmates and the instructor to review at a later time. Students interact with peers and their instructor by reading and commenting on each others' posts. Although communication is delayed in asynchronous CMC, responses tend to be of higher quality, as learners have more time to think about their responses (Davidson-Shivers, Tanner and Muilenburg 2000). Asynchronous e-learning allows students to progress through training at their own pace. This feature can improve motivation for some learners, as those who are advanced can rapidly progress through modules without having to wait for learners who need more time to understand the information.

However, not all asynchronous training is facilitated by an instructor. Some asynchronous e-learning is self-instructional, meaning that students are given the instructional material and access to resources such as electronic books, electronic tutors, and training objectives. Although this can be seen as a disadvantage (as learners have no human instructors to ask questions of), it also offers a major advantage. Self-instructional asynchronous e-learning allows an organization to deliver training to one learner or one million learners with minimal additional costs.

Blended Learning

Blended learning refers to using two types of learning environments in combination to achieve a learning outcome. The very foundation of aviation training, combining both ground school and in-aircraft lessons, is an example of blended learning. Within the realm of e-learning, stand-alone synchronous or asynchronous approaches do not always meet the needs of learners or instructors. Therefore, a combination of e-learning (either synchronous or asynchronous) and traditional classroom instruction is often used. This kind of blended learning environment is sometimes also referred to as a hybrid course. Some aeronautical universities have recently introduced blended learning courses. These blended courses are taught in a traditional classroom setting with some students sitting F2F with their instructor. Through use of digital cameras and microphones installed in the classroom, the class is streamed live online. Through an electronic portal, students in remote locations synchronously connect to the class. In this manner, the e-learning students are able to observe the instructor and discussions among classmates. In addition, groups of remote learners can gather in brick-and-mortar classrooms with computers equipped with webcams and microphones, so that an instructor can teach four or five sections of a class simultaneously while being physically present in one of the classrooms and monitoring the others electronically. When the classrooms are within driving distance of one another, the instructor may visit each classroom on a rotating basis, so that learners have the benefit of the instructor in-person once every four or five class meetings.

Another application of blended learning is using e-learning to support, not replace, classroom instruction. This approach is popular in universities, where instructors post important messages, files, and grades through an online classroom. Students remotely log in to the online classroom whenever they need additional resources to supplement what they have learned in class. The online classroom can also support forums, where students can communicate with each other to share ideas or resources. Instructors have the ability to generate reports detailing the amount of time each student has spent in the online classroom and the resources they accessed. This type of e-learning application is called a learning management system (LMS).

Technology and Characteristics of Modern e-Learning

Technology

Mobile Learning (m-Learning) A relatively new concept in DE technology is mobile learning, also called m-learning. Rather than delivering training via a PC, as is the case with e-learning, m-learning delivers training directly to the learner's handheld mobile device (such as a mobile phone, smartphone, or personal digital assistant (PDA)). m-Learning may take many forms, including blogs, podcasting (an audio or video broadcast that is downloaded for playback), sharing images for supervision purposes, short message service (SMS, that is, text messaging) for collaborative communication, quizzes based in Java, camera-phone communication with instructors and peers, and GPS field trips (Duncan-Howell and Lee 2007). Although the concept of mobile telephone-based training may seem foreign to many in the upper echelons of aviation organizations, modern students are both familiar with and fluent in new technologies. It has been argued that the present educational system has not been designed to teach the students of today, who are 'digital natives' (Prensky 2001). Modern-day students integrate mobile technology into many aspects of their daily lives, including text messaging, blogging, and e-mailing digital pictures and videos. m-Learning attempts to capitalize on student familiarity with mobile technology, delivering training that has been specifically designed for use on wireless mobile devices (WMDs). There are several advantages of delivering training on WMDs, including:

- *Portability*. The small size and long battery life of WMDs makes them a more attractive delivery method than PCs or laptops.
- *Familiarity*. The number of WMDs is continually rising; in fact, the number of mobile telephones (181.1 million) surpassed the number of landlines (177.9 million) in the United States in 2004 (Wagner and Wilson 2005).
- *The digital divide* refers to the gap between people who have access to information and communication technology, and those who do not. The digital divide is an important issue with e-learning, as students must have access to a relatively modern PC in order to access training. However, m-learning sidesteps the digital divide, as WMDs are already accessible by most people (Duncan-Howell and Lee 2007). This is particularly true in parts of the world where mobile devices are much more prolific than landlines, such as parts of Africa and Asia (Brown 2005).

However, there are also disadvantages associated with delivering training on a WMD, such as:

- *Text size*. Small screen size may make reading a challenge, particularly for older learners. However, this is obviously not a factor for training content delivered via auditory broadcasts.

- *Pedagogy*. It is not yet known which theoretical approach to m-learning results in the most efficient training.
- *Compatibility*. Similar to early CBT, there are significant problems with technological compatibility. Delivery of m-learning will be limited until a common platform that supports rich learning applications is developed (Roschelle 2003).

Although m-learning is a relatively new concept, it does have potential to improve the convenience of learning and further promote a shift from teacher-centered to learner-centered instruction. Although m-learning is a tool available to instructional designers, there are many unanswered questions regarding the effectiveness of this delivery method.

Learning Management Systems (LMS) An LMS is a platform that allows an entire organization to manage, create, and track e-learning. In addition, LMSs usually connect several departments of an organization, including scheduling, accounting, and human resources, to streamline course management and automate the cost of training (Hall 2003). LMSs have been a popular e-learning tool for many years, because they offer tremendous flexibility of use and do not require any computer programming skills to operate. LMSs are not mandatory for e-learning course management, but they help in both the design and administration of training. This kind of platform enables instructors to upload their PowerPoint slides and video content to create asynchronous training material; schedule web-based seminars or F2F meetings; and facilitate student discussions through forums, instant messaging software, or whiteboards (which allow groups of online learners to sketch pictures and share them with one another electronically). Instructors can also track learner involvement by generating individual or class activity reports. All of these functions are accessed with a straightforward point-and-click system. Examples of popular LMSs include WebCT or Blackboard. Hall (2003) identifies several important characteristics to consider when choosing an LMS:

- *Availability*. LMSs should be continually accessible 24/7 by thousands of people within an organization, including instructors, students, and administrators simultaneously.
- *Scalability*. In order to accommodate future growth, an LMS must be able to adjust to increasing numbers of students.
- *Usability*. Material and usability must be human-friendly and intuitive.
- *Technology interoperability*. LMSs must support content from several sources and learning standards (such as those outlined by the AICC and the Shareable Content Object Reference Model (SCORM)).
- *Security*. LMSs must allow an organization to limit and control access to e-learning content and back-end functions.

Piskurich (2006) explains that the best approach to choosing an LMS is to keep it as simple as possible. An organization should first determine what it needs from an LMS, and then choose one that best meets those needs. The best LMS will not be installed on individual computers, but exist entirely on a single server. In addition, it should be usable by instructors with little to no training.

Rapid repurposing Many software packages on the market, such as LMSs, help organizations develop effective e-learning programs. However, there is a category of development tools to be wary of: software used for rapid repurposing. Repurposing, or rapid e-learning, involves the creation of an online course by cutting and pasting content that was designed for classroom-based use. Although the result will be deliverable online, it probably won't have the interactions, evaluations, or design necessary for effective e-learning. For e-learning to be effective, it must be based on a thorough analysis that includes performance measurement, task analysis, and the writing of clear objectives. Although the classroom course that the repurposed course is based on may be a good course, the original course may not have begun with a strong analysis. In addition, simply converting PowerPoint slides to e-learning is eliminating all of the interactions, discussions, and activities that occur in the classroom and are facilitated by the instructor. Designing e-learning that works takes expertise, imagination, and time—all in large amounts (Piskurich 2006). In general, stay away from software that makes claims of repurposing PowerPoint slides to an asynchronous online training course in a short period of time. This isn't to suggest that repurposing is impossible, just that it is not an immediate cut-and-paste process.

Characteristics

Self-pacing A popular issue in asynchronous e-learning is whether or not to give learners the ability to control the pace of instruction. All learners will have experience with the Internet, which is the ultimate example of self-controlled learning. The Internet allows users complete freedom to choose-and-click any items they are interested in. Self-pacing within asynchronous e-learning incorporates these navigational elements into training. Self-pacing allows learners to control the following attributes:

- *Content sequence.* The order of lessons, and content within a lesson, can be chosen. This option is often presented as a drop-down table of contents menu that allows the learner to choose which portion of the training to review.
- *Pacing.* In almost all asynchronous e-learning, learners are permitted to spend as much or as little time as they want on each screen within a lesson. It is also common to provide navigation buttons, including rewind, pause/play, fast forward, and main menu.

- *Access to support.* Different e-learning programs vary in the amount of control that learners have in regard to reviewing learning materials. In some training programs, all of the instructional components deemed necessary are integrated into the main instruction program, eliminating the need for additional resources. This is a good option with a homogenous group of learners; however, if learners vary significantly in their level of expertise, the more experienced learners may become bored with reviews and with definitions they already know. In this case, it is helpful to incorporate support that novice learners can review and expert learners can turn off. Examples of support include coach characters, reference materials (books, performance charts, dictionary, glossary of terms), and example cases (adapted from Clark and Mayer 2008).

Ultimately, self-pacing places a portion of instructional design into the hands of the learners. The question is whether learners make appropriate instructional decisions. How aware are learners of what they actually know (Clark and Mayer 2008)? This is a crucial consideration in self-pacing, because learners may think they know 95 percent of the information describing how a jet engine operates. A test on this topic may reveal that they actually know only 45 percent. In general, actual knowledge is not well calibrated to predicted knowledge (Eva et al. 2004). Poor calibration may cause learners to misuse self-paced instruction, skipping over training they need because they assume they already possess the knowledge.

However, learners tend to prefer self-pacing, so this type of instruction might lead to a higher level of motivation (Clark and Mayer 2008). In general, self-pacing is a good instructional strategy for skill-based (rather than cognitive) learning, for novices with minimal previous experience, and when there is access to support control but not content control (Kraiger and Jerden 2007). When self-pacing does not fit with the instruction being designed, another option that tailors the training to each individual is adaptive e-learning.

Adaptive e-Learning All learners are different. Each individual has a different level of expertise, motivation, and capacity for learning. Yet, most instruction is designed as one-size-fits-all. This approach makes sense when a single instructor is teaching a room full of students, as it would be impossible to adapt the difficulty and rate of delivery to each learner's unique level. However, with e-learning, adaptive instruction is a feasible approach. Adaptive instruction can be considered intelligent e-learning, as the training program automatically increases or decreases the level of difficulty according to the learner's correct or incorrect responses and/ or time spent completing activities. Adaptive e-learning can also be customized to support different types of learners. Forty-four percent of pilots are tactile learners, rather than visual or auditory learners (Raisinghani et al. 2005). Adaptive e-learning can modify its presentation to best accommodate such a learning style.

There are four types of adaptive control, based on how the training program is altered in response to the learner's actions (adapted from Clark and Mayer 2008):

1. *Static branching.* On the basis of the result of a single (static) pretest, static branching assigns an e-learning lesson. The e-learning lesson itself does not change in response to performance within the session.
2. *Dynamic branching.* In response to correct or incorrect responses throughout the e-learning lesson, the training content increases or decreases in difficulty. On an air traffic control (ATC) task, researchers found that the final test identified equal performance between students who completed training with dynamic adaptive control and those who completed training according to a fixed predetermined sequence. However, the dynamic adaptive control lesson was completed with an average of ten tasks, whereas the fixed lesson took an average of 20 tasks to complete (Salden et al. 2004). Therefore, dynamic adaptive control may result in a higher efficiency of training.
3. *Adaptive advisement.* Rather than the e-learning program automatically adjusting the difficulty of training, in adaptive advisement the program generates advice for the learner according to his or her performance. This advice may include suggestions about what actions the learner could have taken, how to improve, or an appropriate sequence for learning or practice. This method of adaptive e-learning leaves the learner in control, as he or she is free to accept or reject the advice. Research suggests that this method of training can motivate learners to spend more time studying and practicing, leading to better results on far-transfer tasks (Bell and Kozlowski 2002), which allow students to adapt to new situations (Royer 1979).
4. *Shared control.* In this type of adaptive e-learning, some automatic decisions are based on the learner's performance. For example, the training program will automatically assign a more or less difficult unit of instruction. However, once this has been assigned, the learner is given self-pacing control and is free to pick and choose among topics and activities to complete the unit (Clark and Mayer 2008).

Overall, adaptive instruction is an important feature of e-learning that instructional designers should utilize appropriately. It is important to keep in mind that incorporating adaptive instruction increases the cost and time required to create the training programs, as multiple scenarios, exercises, scripts, and assessments must be created for each level of instruction provided. However, as with all instructional design choices, the decision to incorporate adaptive e-learning must be based on how this feature may help accomplish learning objectives.

Fostering collaboration and learning communities In everyday life, each individual associates with various communities of practice. Communities of practice develop around topics that a group of people, informally connected to one another, find important. For example, as a flight instructor you come across a problem that you don't know the answer to, so you send a quick e-mail to Bob, Charlie, and Sally. You have known all three of them for several years, as they were your fellow students in your first ground school class; however, they currently work at other schools and have their own specialities. You respect all of them and trust that they will be interested in helping you answer your question. This network of people, who you happened to unofficially connect with, is one of your communities of practice. These communities form within businesses, across business units, and across company boundaries. One individual may be associated with several communities of practice surrounding different topics, personally and professionally (Wenger 1998).

Communities of practice are an important consideration in the design of e-learning, because learning does not take place inside a vacuum. For better or worse, learning is inextricably linked to the context within which it is taught. Examples of the knowledge that exists within a community of practice might include how a specific aircraft handles at altitude, the peculiarities of certain passengers or ground crew, or an organization's safety culture. Effective training design requires an understanding that knowledge is 'created, shared, organized, revised, and passed on within and among these communities' (Wenger 1998: 5). A traditional F2F classroom often spawns a community of practice among students, even though the course designer might not have planned for such an effect. Opportunities for students to interact, whether during group projects or spontaneous coffee breaks, allow for communities to form. A major limitation of many e-learning courses is that they are completed in isolation and therefore lack community development opportunities. This is an important consideration in the aviation industry, where team communication and coordination is such a vital component of safe and efficient operations.

Given the importance of facilitating communities of practice, effective e-learning should incorporate activities that promote the formation of a learning community. It is important that the instructor and other students be perceived as human beings, who have a breadth of knowledge and experiences. Some courseware design features can promote community building. For example, in a fully online course, the instructor and students should maintain a personal and professional profile that includes a picture. This allows other students to view class participants as real people. Instructors and course designers can also promote communities of practice by making learner-to-learner interaction mandatory. This is often accomplished through group projects or forum posting assignments (for example, 'Read and comment on the posts of at least 3 other learners').

e-Learning for nontechnical (soft-skill) training A challenge on the horizon of e-learning is its use for soft-skill training (also referred to as nontechnical skills, of which CRM is an example in aviation). Researchers and aviation trainers have raised questions about e-learning being a viable approach to nontechnical training, as the goals of this type of training often focus on communication or workload management skills. Nontechnical topics are typically taught F2F, and there is some debate over whether e-learning provides the interaction necessary to accomplish the desired learning outcomes (Derouin, Fritzsche and Salas 2005). However, early empirical research into the feasibility of asynchronous e-learning for single-pilot resource management skills demonstrated that situation awareness skills were significantly better after training (Kearns, in press). The application of e-learning to nontechnical training is explored in more detail in Chapter 5.

Conclusion

e-Learning has a history filled with overhyped courses that underperformed. Although technology will always outpace research, modern e-learning has progressed to the point where a sound foundation of principles and practice exists. The various characteristics, technologies, and delivery methods (synchronous, asynchronous, blended learning, m-learning) of e-learning will facilitate a continual increase in our ability to efficiently accomplish the learning objectives of pilot training programs.

Practical Summary

- e-Learning is a shortened form of the term *electronic learning*.
- Early e-learning was called *computer-based training* (CBT) and was characterized by CD-ROM based software:
  - CBT was plagued by incompatibility, high development costs, and poor instructional design.
- The Internet revolutionized the delivery of e-learning.
- There are several modern e-learning delivery methods:
  - synchronous, which involves instructors and students in online classes simultaneously at predetermined times;
  - asynchronous, in which students log into online classes whenever it is convenient for them, at any time;
  - blended learning, which entails a combination of approaches, typically classroom instruction combined with either synchronous or asynchronous e-learning;
  - mobile learning (m-learning), in which training materials are delivered to a learner's wireless mobile device (WMD), such as a mobile telephone.
- Several technologies are important to modern e-learning, including:
  - learning management systems (LMSs), learning platforms that allow multiple users within an organization to create, organize, and track learning;
  - rapid repurposing software, which claim to convert currently taught classes into e-learning in a matter of hours or days;
    - be wary of repurposing software, as it only directly converts classroom training to e-learning without capitalizing on the benefits of online delivery.

- There are also several characteristics that are important to modern e-learning, including:
  - self-pacing, which allows learners to control the content and rate of delivery of e-learning;
  - adaptive e-learning, within which the content of the training program adjusts difficulty level in accordance with the learner's correct or incorrect answers;
  - fostering e-learning collaboration among learners to promote learning communities;
  - challenges of delivering nontechnical training (such as CRM) via e-learning.

Chapter 3
Does e-Learning Work?

> It's fine to celebrate success, but it is more important to heed the lessons of failure.
> —Bill Gates

Overview

The purpose of this chapter is to discuss the effectiveness of e-learning (compared to traditional classroom instruction), by:

- reviewing the no-significant-difference debate, in which:
  - one side argues that the instructional delivery method used (e-learning or classroom instruction) doesn't matter, as the content is more important than the delivery method
  - the other side argues that e-learning incorporates features that improve learning and that are not possible in a classroom environment;
- reviewing several meta-analyses that compare the effectiveness of e-learning with traditional classroom instruction.

Introduction

Recently, TransAsia Airways (which is a domestic airline in Taiwan) developed and integrated into its operations a major e-learning program, with about 80 hours of instruction distributed among 60 e-learning modules. Overall, the training was associated with the following opportunity costs:

- saved roughly 340,000 USD on flight crew salaries by decreasing training time and increasing flying time;
- increased operational earnings by roughly 840,000 USD, since they were able to schedule additional flights;
- saved roughly 20,000 USD on salaries for lecturers;
- spent roughly 400,000 USD on e-learning expenses, including course development, infrastructure construction, a learning management system (LMS), e-learning websites, and so on.

Overall, the implementation of e-learning has saved the airline 800,000 USD each year (Chuang et al. 2008).

Although most airlines would be eager to reap these benefits, the savings associated with e-learning are unimportant if the training does not accomplish the desired learning outcomes. Therefore, it is important to review the e-learning research to determine how effective this method of training is, compared to classroom instruction. In addition, it is necessary to identify the characteristics of e-learning that result in improved learning outcomes.

Effectiveness of e-Learning

This chapter focuses on the effectiveness of e-learning. The issue of how e-learning produces knowledge, skills, and attitudes compared to classroom instruction will be explored through a review of academic literature. In addition, guidelines regarding attributes that increase the effectiveness of e-learning will be identified. Unfortunately, in the real world, time and financial pressures often result in the development of e-learning simply because the technology is available and there is a need. The purpose of this chapter is to provide guidelines to help organizational decision-makers determine whether e-learning is a feasible option for their training needs, or if another delivery method (such as blended learning) might be more appropriate. In addition, the chapter will identify best practices for e-learning courses as discussed in the literature.

It is clear that a heated debate exists around the effectiveness of e-learning compared to classroom instruction. One side states that it is illogical to perform comparative research assessing the differences between e-learning and classroom instruction, because it is the content of instruction that impacts learning, rather than the delivery method itself (Clark 1994). The counterargument is that because e-learning provides instructional opportunities that are not feasible or practical in a classroom setting—such as adaptive instruction and immediate feedback—comparative research is indeed warranted. The debate continues, although current articles have shifted the focus away from basing broad conclusions on individual studies, and toward meta-analyses that systematically investigate research articles meeting predetermined criteria.

The No-Significant-Difference Debate

Ruth E. Clark (1983, 1994) is the most notable of the researchers who maintain that e-learning and classroom instruction are 'mere vehicles that deliver instruction but do not influence student achievement any more than the truck that delivers our groceries causes changes in our nutrition' (Clark 1983: 445). According to Clark, there is nothing particularly advantageous about computer-based delivery, and any training can provide excellent instruction if it is appropriately designed. Therefore, computer-based and classroom delivery are of practically equal value, and the decision to choose one over another should be based on managerial factors (such as cost, instructor availability, and worker preference) rather than on learning factors.

This perspective has received wide support (Bernard et al. 2004; Russell 1999, 2009). Russell's (2009) work is particularly convincing, as it indexes and summarizes 355 research reports, from 1928 until 2008, and presents evidence of there being no-significant-differences in student outcomes between classroom and distance education (DE). However, there have been rebuttals of Russell's perspective. For example, Machtmes and Asher (2000) pointed out that many of the studies referenced in Russell's (1999) work are not experimental; they are surveys with small sample sizes and no mention of learner demographics or survey return rate.

The counterargument to the no-significant-difference approach is that e-learning allows for innovative instructional design practices that are not feasible in a classroom setting. For example, e-learning enables worldwide training that learners can access when job requirements allow; it can also reduce information overload, adapt to the skill level of individual employees, and provide immediate feedback (Goldstein and Ford 2002; Kulik and Kulik 1988; Welsh et al. 2003). All of these characteristics are extremely difficult to reproduce in a classroom setting. However, even considering some of the unique capabilities of e-learning, the question of whether it produces similar or improved learning over classroom instruction remains. In addition, from an organizational perspective, e-learning is only viable for professional training if learning transfers to the operational environment, is well accepted by learners, and is cost-effective for the organization (Sitzmann et al. 2006). Therefore, it is important to review the meta-analyses in the field to gain some perspective on e-learning effectiveness.

The Effectiveness of e-Learning vs. Classroom Instruction: Meta-Analyses

There are literally hundreds of published studies comparing DE to classroom-based training. However, because of the wide variability in course content, learner demographics, delivery methodology, and instructional media, it is not appropriate to make a broad generalization regarding e-learning effectiveness after reviewing a single study. For this reason, meta-analyses are used to explore trends that are evident across several studies (Sitzman et al. 2006). Meta-analyses are a valid and reliable method of synthesizing a large body of literature, because they utilize a systematic process and specific criteria to identify and select applicable research articles, and a verified statistical procedure for analyzing the results (Zhao et al. 2005). Several meta-analyses that assess the comparative effectiveness of various forms of DE and traditional classroom instruction have been published.

A meta-analysis by Kulik and Kulik (1991) focused on whether computer-based instruction (CBI) enhanced learning, as evidenced by increases in final examination scores. It is important to note that CBI differs from a modern understanding of e-learning. CBI is a much broader term, encompassing any computer-based educational tools, used either within a classroom to supplement a lecture or asynchronously from a home computer. Kulik and Kulik reviewed 254 studies and concluded that CBI raised examination scores by 0.30 standard deviations, from the 50th percentile to the 62nd. They also found that the duration of the instruction was strongly related to the size of the effect, with CBI being especially effective when the training was four weeks or less. In these shorter courses, CBI raised final examination performance by 0.42 standard deviations. A possible explanation for this increase is the novelty effect—whereby learners work harder because of the freshness of the training—which wears off over time. Kulik and Kulik also determined that learners enjoyed their training somewhat more when CBI was utilized.

More than a decade later, Bernard et al. (2004) conducted a meta-analysis of 232 comparative studies on distance and classroom-based education, published between 1985 and 2002, to determine whether a significant difference existed. They hypothesized that good instruction, regardless of delivery method, should result in equal learning outcomes. This hypothesis supports Clark's (1994) no-significant-difference hypothesis, which was discussed previously. However, Bernard and colleagues also posited that if the DE delivery method allows learners to become more engaged through constructive techniques, a significant difference may be evident: 'In [distance education], media may transform the learning experience in ways that are unanticipated and not regularly available in face-to-face instructional situations' (Bernard et al. 2004: 382).

The results of Bernard and colleagues' (2004) investigation revealed that overall, no signficant differences were present between student outcomes in DE and classroom-based education. There was, however, wide variability among both DE courses and classroom-based courses. These results mirror those of Cavanaugh (2001), who conducted a meta-analysis of 19 studies that compared test results of Kindergarten to Grade 12 students who had received either classroom instruction or instruction using interactive DE technology. The weighted mean effect size was 0.147 with a standard deviation of 0.69; in other words, Cavanaugh's results also indicate a wide variability between studies. The results of these two studies suggest that although the majority of DE courses resulted in the same outcomes as classroom-based courses, some distance courses performed either much better or much worse than their classroom counterparts.

When the results were further separated to distinguish between synchronous and asynchronous instruction, asynchronous courses produced better performance than classroom courses, while synchronous courses performed more poorly (Bernard et al. 2004). Bernard and colleagues presented several possible reasons for this finding, including the perspective that synchronous e-learning may be a 'poorer quality replication of classroom instruction; there is neither the flexibility of scheduling and place of learning nor the individual attention that exists in many applications of asynchronous [distance education]' (Bernard et al. 2004: 408).

Whereas previous works had assessed the comparative effectiveness of the delivery methods, Zhao and colleagues (2005) completed a systematic analysis of practical guidelines for improving the quality of DE. From their meta-analysis of 51 research articles comparing DE and traditional classroom learning outcomes, they identified seven broad findings:

1. Not all DE programs are created equal.
2. Interaction is key to effective DE, whether that interaction occurs with the instructor, other learners, or the instructional media.
3. Live human instructors are important, as the degree of instructor involvement influences course effectiveness.
4. A mixture of asynchronous e-learning and face-to-face (F2F) interaction results in the best learning (although the F2F interaction may be conducted via computer conferencing).
5. Course content is a factor in the effectiveness of e-learning.
6. Learner characteristics impact the effectiveness of e-learning.
7. The effectiveness of e-learning has been improving over time (Zhao et al. 2005).

Tallent-Runnels and colleagues (2006) conducted a literature review of online teaching and learning research. Broadly, the authors determined that asynchronous communication facilitated high-quality communication, although it did not surpass traditional classroom communication. In addition, learners (and instructors) can be challenged by the skills required for participation in e-learning. Therefore, learners with previous experience in computers are more satisfied with e-learning. Lastly, self-pacing within e-learning is important; students appreciate the opportunity to progress through a course at their own rate.

In 2006, Sitzmann et al. conducted another meta-analytic review of e-learning relative to traditional classroom instruction. One of the significant factors of their review was an analysis of how each delivery method impacted the declarative and procedural knowledge gained by learners.

Declarative knowledge refers to the learner's memory of the concepts and details presented in training and how knowledge elements relate to each other (Kraiger, Ford and Salas 1993). Learning outcomes of declarative knowledge include changes in how knowledge is structured and strategies for applying the knowledge. Declarative knowledge can be thought of as 'knowledge of' something (Norman 2002). An example of declarative knowledge is a pilot's ability to recite a particular regulation.

Procedural knowledge refers to specific details about how to perform a task. Procedural learning outcomes consist of compilation (mentally grouping and proceduralizing steps into a complex structure) and automaticity (completing tasks automatically without conscious effort, which allows for better performance on supplementary tasks). Procedural knowledge can be thought of as 'knowledge how' to do something (Norman 2002). An example of procedural knowledge would be any standard operating procedure (SOP) a pilot knows, such as how to complete a preflight walkaround check.

Overall, Sitzmann et al. (2006) determined that e-learning was 6 percent more effective than traditional classroom instruction for the teaching of declarative knowledge. Both instructional delivery methods were equally effective for teaching procedural knowledge, and learners were equally satisfied with the two methods.

Sitzmann et al. (2006) also addressed the question of blended learning. For teaching job-relevant knowledge and skills, blended learning was more effective than traditional classroom instruction alone. For declarative knowledge, blended instruction was 13 percent more effective than classroom instruction alone; for procedural knowledge, blended instruction was 20 percent more effective (Sitzmann et al. 2006). Zhao and colleagues (2005) drew a similar conclusion; their meta-analysis demonstrated that learning outcomes for blended instruction were higher than for traditional classroom instruction or e-learning alone. A Thomson NETg (2002) study involving 128 participants confirmed the results of these meta-analyses. This investigation compared students who completed a blended learning course with students who conducted only asynchronous training; the results indicated that the blended learners performed real-world tasks 41 percent faster and with 30 percent more accuracy than the asynchronous e-learning group.

Conclusion

The results of several meta-analytic reviews indicate that the no-significant-difference argument does not fully answer the question of whether e-learning or classroom instruction results in better learning outcomes. In general, classroom courses and e-learning courses (with identical content and exercises) produce the same learning outcomes. However, some e-learning courses significantly outperform or underperform classroom instruction (Bernard et al. 2004; Cavanaugh 2001). Thus it appears that instructional designers who capitalize on the features of e-learning can produce courses that result in better learning outcomes than classroom instruction. However, it must be remembered that some e-learning courses have resulted in significantly worse learning outcomes than classroom instruction. Perhaps the enthusiasm of early e-learning developers 'produced too many new ventures pushing too many untested products—products that, in their initial form, turned out not to deliver as much value as promised. . . . The hard fact is that e-learning took off before people really knew how to use it' (Zemsky and Massy 2004: iii). Clearly, the effectiveness of any e-learning course will be directly linked to how the course is designed. Instructional design for e-learning in aviation will be explored step-by-step later in this book.

Practical Summary

- In general, if an e-learning course is developed with instructional content identical to that of a classroom-based course, one can expect no significant

differences in learning outcomes between the courses.
- Some e-learning courses perform much better and some perform much worse than classroom courses:
  - instructional design that capitalizes on the capabilities of e-learning (such as interactivity and immediate feedback) results in better learning;
  - it is unlikely that quickly developed e-learning courses that have identical content to classroom courses, will result in improved learning;
  - asynchronous e-learning results in better learning than synchronous e-learning.
- Blended learning, which incorporates both e-learning and face-to-face (F2F) instruction, results in better learning than either synchronous or asynchronous delivery alone.
- e-Learning should incorporate the use of live human instructors to communicate with learners, either synchronously or asynchronously.
- e-Learning is more effective than classroom instruction for teaching declarative knowledge, and it is equally effective for procedural knowledge.

Chapter 4
Foundational e-Learning Theories

> He who loves practice without theory is like the sailor who boards ship without a rudder and compass and never knows where he may cast.
>
> —Leonardo da Vinci

Overview

The purpose of this chapter is to introduce the reader to some important theories that impact the design and effectiveness of e-learning. This chapter presents:

- an overview of the cognitive approach to learning—including how the human memory system processes and retains information—and cognitive load theory;
- the constructivist perspective on learning, which explains that new knowledge is learned by connecting concepts to previous knowledge and is therefore a unique process for each individual;
- an introduction to expert performance research, which explains how expertise develops and the expertise reversal effect;
- an explanation of intrinsic and extrinsic motivation;
- a review of the apprenticeship approach, and a discussion of how a cognitive apprenticeship approach is suitable to e-learning in aviation.

Introduction

There is a massive body of work describing theories about how people process information and eventually develop the knowledge, skills, and attitudes to become experts. The purpose of this chapter is not to provide a comprehensive review of this body of work, but to highlight key theories that directly impact the instructional design of effective e-learning. Although practitioners may be keen to move on to the instructional design part of this book, the information in this chapter should be reviewed first. This chapter can be thought of as the groundwork upon which subsequent chapters are built.

The topics in this chapter include an overview of the human memory system and cognitive load theory (CLT), the constructivist approach to learning, expert performance and the expertise reversal effect, and lastly the cognitive apprenticeship approach to aviation training.

The Three Learning Domains

All learning can be broadly categorized into three domains: cognitive, psychomotor, or affective (Reigeluth 1999). Cognitive learning, the most widely understood domain, is concerned with the storing of new information in the learner's long-term memory. Within pilot training curriculums, cognitive learning typically applies during ground-school lessons in a classroom. A detailed overview of the cognitive approach to learning is presented later in this chapter. Before continuing, however, it is important to define the psychomotor and affective learning domains as well.

Psychomotor learning refers to the learner's ability to perform hands-on skills. Psychomotor instruction is an important aspect of pilot training, typically occurring in an aircraft or flight simulator. Within aviation, an apprenticeship approach to psychomotor learning is utilized; students work with an instructor, observing and practicing skills until they are capable of performing maneuvers independently.

Affective learning refers to the appropriate attitudes and emotions associated with a particular environment. Although affective learning may not immediately seem as important to pilot training curriculums as cognitive and psychomotor learning, appropriate attitudes have been linked to safety within the aviation environment (Helmreich, Merritt and Wilhelm 1999). Pilot training courses that target affective learning may include crew resource management (CRM) or safety culture training.

In the aviation industry in particular, success is highly dependent upon the learner's ability to master skills in all three domains. Although the terms *cognitive*, *psychomotor*, and *affective* are not commonly used in the industry, it is common to hear of pilots who have the 'book smarts,' or cognitive abilities, but not the 'hands and feet,' or psychomotor abilities. Likewise, a working knowledge of affective attributes is what allows a ground-school instructor to quickly recognize which learners in a classroom are the 'show-offs' and which ones have professional attitudes.

When designing an e-learning program or course, it is important to understand which aspect of learning the training is meant to target. Learning is not the automatic result of instruction; the program or course must be carefully and strategically designed to meet the needs of the learner and the organization. Design tips for targeting cognitive, psychomotor, and affective learning are included in Chapter 8.

Cognitive Approach to Learning

CLT is a learning theory that describes how learning occurs. The limitations of the human memory system provide the basic premise of CLT.

The Human Memory System

Human memory consists of two parts: working memory (WM) and long-term memory (LTM). Humans utilize WM whenever they are actively processing or rehearsing information. Therefore, whenever people are deliberately trying to learn new information they are utilizing their WM. However, WM is limited in duration; information in WM is short-lived, meaning that once you stop working with and rehearsing the information you will forget it.

In addition, WM is limited in capacity. Miller (1956) determined that the capacity of WM is seven chunks of information, plus or minus two, and that any additional information will create an overload situation and slow down information processing. Where this gets complicated is in defining what constitutes a chunk of information. For example, an individual's telephone number constitutes one chunk of information, even though it contains ten numbers. However, if a stranger is required to remember the same telephone number, it may be ten chunks of information. One's facility in chunking several pieces of information together is based on experience and organizational ability. Purposely chunking pieces of information together results in the information taking up less space in WM. Organizational strategies that are used to improve memory are called mnemonics.

More recently, Cowan (2000) presented evidence suggesting that the capacity of WM is much less than what Miller (1956) hypothesized, particularly for new and dynamic information. The limitation of WM is actually closer to three or four chunks (Cowan 2000). Regardless of the precise capacity limits of WM, the implication for instructional designers is the same: WM presents a bottleneck in the human memory system, and instruction must be carefully designed to avoid overloading its limitations (Ayres and van Gog 2009).

Through rehearsal, elaboration, and practice within WM, new information will be learned and become a part of one's permanent LTM. LTM, much different from WM, has an almost limitless capacity. LTM represents all of the knowledge and memories that one has collected over a lifetime. Whereas WM refers to information that an individual is actively thinking about, LTM stores inactive information for use at a later time. Ultimately, learning occurs when new information becomes stored in LTM (Wickens et al. 2003). Within an individual's LTM, some memories are organized into schemas. A schema is a mental framework containing all of the information related to a specific topic, such as aviation. The more experience and education an individual has in aviation, the more memories will be associated with the person's aviation schema.

One benefit of memories being organized into schemas is that one schema is often regarded as one chunk of information. Therefore, when utilizing WM, an individual can reference his or her entire aviation schema—which represents an enormous amount of detailed information—while still having WM chunks available for processing new information. Another benefit of schemas is that as individuals become an expert, they are able to process domain-specific schemas automatically, without conscious thought. This phenomenon, which is known as automaticity, further reduces WM load. Thus the cognitive system of an expert is capable of working with complicated material that would appear to an observer as exceeding WM capacity (Paas, Renkl and Sweller 2003). For this reason, expertise is an important consideration in the design of instruction.

Cognitive Load Theory (CLT)

CLT, which originated in the 1980s, focuses on how instruction is impacted by the limitations of WM and the interaction between WM and LTM. There are three components of cognitive load: intrinsic, extraneous, and germane.

As previously discussed, information presented to learners imposes a higher cognitive load if it is complex or new, or if it has interactive elements. Therefore, the nature of the instructional material itself is related to the cognitive load imposed on learners. The cognitive load associated with the inherent complexity of material is called the intrinsic cognitive load. The intrinsic cognitive load cannot be reduced unless the learning task can be broken down and simplified (Paas, Renkl and Sweller 2003).

Researchers have also determined that regardless of course material, cognitive load can be impacted by the manner in which information is presented and by the instructional activities used. Cognitive load imposed by the poor instructional design of a course is called extraneous cognitive load (Paas, Renkl and Sweller 2003). For an example of an instructional activity that would cause extraneous cognitive load, consider the following scenario: Learners are asked to learn a new standard operating procedure (SOP) that is related to the weather. However, in this particular course, the weather information is not presented and the learners are required to search out the weather information while holding the new SOP in WM. Maintaining information in WM while searching for supplementary information causes a high cognitive load. The design of this activity, rather than the material itself, is likely to overload the learners' WM.

The third component of CLT, germane cognitive load, is also impacted by the instructional design of the course. However, germane cognitive load is the opposite of extraneous cognitive load, as it enhances rather than interferes with learning. Ultimately, an instructional designer should try to reduce extraneous load to make WM capacity available for germane cognitive load. Examples of instructional activities that contribute to germane cognitive load include step-by-step examples, activities that require self-explanations, practice that encourages automaticity of new skills, and mental rehearsal of complicated material (Clark, Nguyen and Sweller 2006). Instructional activities that cause germane cognitive load promote the acquisition, organization, and automation of schemas (Paas, Renkl and Sweller 2003).

If learning is to occur, these three forms of cognitive load—intrinsic, extraneous, and germane—cannot exceed a learner's WM capacity. The intrinsic load is constant, and is based on the complexity of the material presented. Any

WM resources remaining while the intrinsic load is being processed can be applied toward extraneous or germane cognitive load. Furthermore, any reduction in extraneous load makes room for additional resources to be dedicated towards germane cognitive load. An instructional designer's attention to this area leads to instruction that more effectively promotes schema acquisition and automaticity, thereby reducing the intrinsic load of the material. This process creates a cycle through which a learner develops detailed schemas that are referenced automatically, resulting in the learning of increasingly complex skills and knowledge (Paas, Renkl and Sweller 2003).

CLT is an important learning theory that has directly contributed to instructional design guidelines. One of the tenets of CLT is that the development of schemas in LTM is essential to the development of expertise and problem-solving capabilities in learners (Ayres and van Gog 2009).

Constructivism

According to the constructivist view of learning, individuals create their own perspectives on and meanings for events. That is, if a person is asked to recall a particular piece of information, that information will be inextricably linked to the individual's experiences with it. For example, if asked a question about an aircraft maneuver such as a spin, a pilot is likely to recall information based on his or her experiences flying the aircraft in a spin maneuver, rather than objective performance data related to spins. Therefore, each individual's understanding and mental organization of a particular piece of knowledge will be unique. So, although learners will be able to share information and work together, the instructor cannot expect their understandings of the information to be identical.

In addition, a person's behavior is influenced by his or her history of experiencing similar situations in the past. A characteristic of human beings is that we are adept at reconstructing and reconceptualizing past experiences in many different ways (Duffy and Jonassen 1992).

Learning is the process of constructing knowledge, not of absorbing it verbatim. Think about a course you have completed. What were the most memorable aspects of the training? Is it easiest to remember specific performance specifications, or do you remember an anecdote told by the instructor that was similar to your own experiences? Constructivism takes the perspective that learning is enhanced when instructors are able to relate new information to individuals' past experiences. Therefore, learning is dependent on an individual's previous knowledge, which can be used to construct new knowledge.

Another characteristic of learning is that it is closely related to the context (environment) within which it is transmitted to the learner (Resnick 1989). According to Brown, Collins and Duguid (1989), 'knowledge is situated, being in part a product of the activity, context, and culture in which it is developed and used' (32). This aspect of learning highlights a key shortcoming of classroom-based lectures. If memory is linked to experiences, how can information delivered in a classroom setting be applied to real-world situations? The significant differences between classroom training and real-world situations are a major reason for the low transfer of training between these environments (Brown, Collins and Duguid 1989; Resnick 1987). Therefore, at a minimum, instructors should incorporate real-world scenarios and examples into their training programs to provide examples of how the knowledge can be applied in the real world. For this reason, as we shall see later in this chapter, a cognitive apprenticeship approach has potential learning advantages over traditional classroom approaches. Ultimately, from a constructivist perspective, the goal of instruction is to provide the contexts and support that individuals require to understand new information and apply that knowledge to the situations and scenarios they encounter in the real-world (Duffy and Jonassen 1992).

Expertise

Expert performance research investigates how experts gain skills. However, translating the mechanisms behind superior performance into instructional recommendations is not a priority of expert performance research (van Gog et al. 2005).

Expert Performance Research

Experts are characterized by close to error-free performance on domain-specific tasks, enhanced short-term and LTM, and improved understandings of problem scenarios (Chi, Glaser and Farr 1988). Expert performance research attempts to understand the mechanisms that allow experts to have consistently superior performance on domain-specific tasks (Ericsson and Lehmann 1996). This body of work has determined that the acquisition of expert performance does not equate directly to how much experience an individual has. Rather, expert performance is directly related to the amount of deliberate practice extended by the learner. Deliberate practice is typically created by an instructor to target specific areas of a task that require improvement. To be effective, deliberate practice activities must be challenging, provide feedback, and allow for refinement (van Gog et al. 2005). Individual differences are closely linked to deliberate practice experience (Ericsson, Krampe and Tesch-Romer 1993). In fact, characteristics that were once believed to be innate abilities, such as skill in sports or chess, may actually be the result of deliberate practice over a minimum of ten years (Ericsson, Krampe and Tesch-Romer 1993). Because this type of practice requires a high level of concentration and is effortful to maintain, it is carried out not for enjoyment but to refine or enhance a specific skill (van Gog et al. 2005).

Expertise Reversal Effect

Clearly, it is important for instructional designers to consider what cognitive load their training will impose on learners. However, identifying the cognitive load imposed by training leads to a secondary challenge, as the expertise of individual learners may vary significantly. Within a single training group, expertise may vary between new hires and experienced professionals who have been with a company for many years. Delivering a standard e-learning training program to the entire group could cause an expertise reversal effect. An expertise reversal effect is what happens when training techniques that are effective with novices are less effective with experts and can even negatively impact expert learners (Kalyuga et al. 2003). For this and other reasons, an analysis of learner characteristics is an important step in the instructional design process.

Expert learners have the advantage of multiple well-organized schemas that allow them to work with an enormous amount of information in their WM. In addition, because of extensive practice, experts can reference some of their schemas automatically, resulting in minimal WM load. Computer-based instruction (CBI) can be designed to present additional guidance for novices who lack these sophisticated schema. The instruction must be designed in consideration of the cognitive load it will impose on learners (Sweller 1999); otherwise, learners will resort to cognitively demanding problem-solving search strategies that result in high WM loads (Kalyuga et al. 2003).

However, if an e-learning course incorporating additional guidance for novices is presented to experts, and the program does not allow them to turn off this feature, the experts receive information from both their individual schemas and the assistance designed for novices (Kalyuga et al. 2003). The resulting integration and cross-referencing of the redundant information sources increases the experts' WM load, eliminating the advantage of having existing schemas. As a consequence, this 'instructional guidance, which may be essential for novices, may have negative consequences for more experienced learners' (Kalyuga et al. 2003: 24). This is an example of the expertise reversal effect in a training program that improves the performance of novices but decreases the performance of experts.

Motivation Theories

Another important area of background theory is human motivation. Motivation theories provide ways of describing the nature of human beings and what causes them to act. Motivation is an important characteristic to consider in the design of instruction, because instructional designers can integrate creative exercises to motivate learning when the course material is inherently complex and dull.

There are two basic categories of motivation: intrinsic and extrinsic (Deci and Ryan 1985). Intrinsic motivation is an individual's drive to learn, according to his or her natural interest or curiosity in a topic. Extrinsic motivation, on the other hand, refers to external influences that drive an individual to learn. Examples of extrinsic pressures may include financial bonuses, employer pressure, or training that is mandatory in order to keep a job or pilot license. Although it would be ideal for every individual within a company to have a high level of intrinsic motivation for every training course, this is not a realistic expectation. The level of intrinsic motivation does not have any relation to the importance of the training. Some very important material is inherently complicated and challenging and is therefore associated with a low level of intrinsic motivation. For this reason, extrinsic motivation is an important aspect of the educational process. Without any extrinsic motivation (such as regulatory guidance), employees would be permitted to complete training whenever they felt like it. Clearly, this would not be an acceptable training philosophy within aviation or any other safety-oriented industry! Therefore, instructional designers must attempt to balance the levels of intrinsic and extrinsic motivation. Conducting an analysis of learners is an important element of the instructional design process, as it provides some indication of what exercises may increase or decrease motivation. Overall, understanding the importance of both intrinsic and extrinsic motivation allows instructional designers to recognize when a course may entail low intrinsic motivation, so that they can integrate interesting challenges, stimulating activities, interactive exercises, or games. Practice activities are discussed in more detail in Chapter 6 and 9.

Cognitive Apprenticeship

The last theory discussed in this overview is that of a cognitive apprenticeship and its potential to improve traditional pilot training. Although the majority of this chapter focuses on ways to improve the classroom component of pilot training, this section provides tips on how to enhance pilot problem-solving and critical-thinking performance during flight training and solo flight.

A problem with classroom-based education is that it is often instructor-centric, or worse, textbook-centric. For example, training may be based on what the instructor feels the learners need to know, or which chapters of a textbook to teach-for-the-test, rather than on what knowledge and skills are actually required for success in the real world.

Historically, most of society's practical training has been conducted through a master–apprentice model. Aviation, although a comparably young industry, is no exception. When an individual seeks to become a pilot, he or she is assigned to an instructor pilot. Until the student pilot has obtained a pilot license, most flight time will be spent observing and working with an instructor. As experience increases, reliance on the instructor decreases, until the necessary knowledge, skills, and attitudes are passed down to allow for safe operation of an aircraft.

This process is identical to the formal description of apprenticeship. Collins, Brown and Newman (1989) describe apprenticeship as a process by which novices learn complex skills within a specific domain through modeling, coaching, and fading. The apprentice observes the expert carrying out a particular skill or maneuver (modeling); then attempts to execute the maneuver under the guidance and supervision of the expert, who provides help when needed (coaching); and lastly the expert reduces their participation to only small hints and minor feedback, and the learner is able to execute the entire maneuver almost independently (fading).

A key benefit of apprenticeship is that the culture of the learning environment matches that of the real-world industry within which the skills must be applied. In addition, the learner often has access to several masters and therefore several models of expertise to demonstrate that there isn't only one way to master a task (Collins, Brown and Newman 1989).

Although the traditional master–apprentice model has served the aviation industry well over the last 100 years, an obvious shortcoming is that a traditional apprenticeship allows for the observation of psychomotor and verbal skills only. Through observing the physical movements and verbal dialogue of the expert instructor, the student is able to develop the skills necessary to maneuver an aircraft and communicate over the radio and with a crewmember successfully. However, there is no guarantee or test to determine whether the student has attained the critical thinking and problem-solving skills necessary to become an expert pilot. Unfortunately, the current industry standard is to measure the expertise of a pilot according to the number of hours he or she has flown. However, this metric provides no guarantee of expertise, as pilots with the same number of hours may have encountered dramatically different experiences and training rigor.

Therefore, it is important for the industry to rethink training and identify processes for training pilots in critical thinking and problem-solving skills. As a continuation of the traditional master–apprentice approach, this training would go one step past the observation of physical and verbal skills and present students with the internal thought processes of experts, making these thoughts visible to the student (Collins, Brown and Holum 2004). This process is called a cognitive apprenticeship, and it represents an opportunity to enrich traditional pilot training.

An important aspect of cognitive apprenticeships is the highlighting of differences between expert and novice problem-solving strategies, which allows learners to identify the differences between their strategies and the ideal, and to make small performance adjustments toward the expert approach (Collins, Brown and Newman 1989). e-Learning provides an effective means for delivering this comparative problem-solving training. For example, videotaped flight scenarios can be presented to learners via a computer. After viewing the scenario, the learners may be given the opportunity to think through the problem that was presented and determine what their response would be. They then type their decision-making process step by step. Once the learners are satisfied with their responses, they are presented with the expert pilot's response for comparison. This method allows the thought process of the expert pilot—a process that was previously invisible to the learner—to become clear, understandable, and functional for learning purposes. A similar e-learning method was used within an US Air Force training program called Sherlock, which was designed to help technicians troubleshoot an F-15 test station. Researchers concluded that 'twenty-five hours of Sherlock practice time produced average improvements that were, in many respects, equivalent to the effects of four years on the job' (Lesgold et al. 1992: 54). An added benefit of cognitive apprenticeships is that the students can be presented with instructionally relevant situations and scenarios that would be either too dangerous for in-aircraft training or rarely encountered during such training (Collins, Brown and Holum 2004).

There are some differences between cognitive apprenticeship and the traditional apprenticeship approach. First, in a traditional apprenticeship, the tasks and challenges that a novice encounters are the result of real-world activities in the workplace. By comparison, cognitive apprenticeship tasks are meant to meet the needs of the learners by slowly increasing in complexity and allowing for practice of new strategies (Collins, Brown and Newman 1989). Second, a cognitive apprenticeship focuses on teaching knowledge that can be applied to multiple novel settings rather than to one particular scenario. The purpose of this approach is to prepare learners for unusual or unexpected situations. Therefore, the instructional design of cognitive apprenticeships should not be based solely on real-world apprenticeship experiences but can use the opportunity to carefully design situations that incrementally increase in complexity and apply to multiple novel situations.

Clark (2003) explains that a cognitive apprenticeship approach is most suitable for far-transfer tasks and building problem-solving skills, and for learners who already have content knowledge—all of which describe requirements of modern aviation training. The cognitive apprenticeship approach requires active constructivist learning, in which knowledge is constructed individually according to the learner's personal interpretations and experiences (Jonassen 1999).

Computer-based pilot training programs, as part of a cognitive apprenticeship, should ask pilot learners to model expert pilot behavior and to articulate their own thought processes and reflect against expert behavior. Such programs should also incorporate a coaching agent to provide tips, and provide an opportunity to explore and practice concepts through simulator-based scenarios (Collins, Brown and Newman 1989). Woolley and Jarvis (2007) argue that a cognitive apprenticeship model effectively prepares students for the operational environment and lays the foundation for the development of a competent practitioner with the physical and cognitive skills required for the job.

Conclusion

This chapter barely scratches the surface of the research available on each of the topics discussed. This introduction to these concepts is offered as a foundation for topics that will be discussed in subsequent chapters.

Although the cognitive and constructive approaches are often regarded as distinct, both are of value to e-learning developers. The cognitive approach highlights the limitations of the human WM system and the importance of targeted instruction and carefully designed interfaces. Constructivism emphasizes the importance of experience-based learning situated within real-world contexts. Although these two approaches are distinct, it is possible to apply both within the design of an e-learning program.

The information regarding expert performance also directly impacts training design. It is important for designers to realize that one-size-fits-all does not necessarily apply to e-learning and that training that improves the skills of novices may have no impact on—and can even deteriorate—the skills of experts! Expert performance research supports the importance of a careful learner analysis within the instructional design process.

Lastly, the history of apprenticeship within aviation was discussed, along with the potential for a cognitive apprenticeship approach within the industry. The goal of cognitive apprenticeship is to build upon the strengths of apprenticeships and to take learning one step further by making expert thought processes visible to learners. Ultimately, this style of training should improve the critical thinking and decision-making skills of pilots.

Practical Summary

- e-Learning theories provide the foundational understanding required to design training programs.
- Broadly, learning exists in three domains: psychomotor, affective, and cognitive:
  - psychomotor refers to hands-on skills;
  - affective refers to appropriate attitudes and emotions;
  - cognitive refers to knowledge and is described by the human memory system and its impact on learning:
    - working memory (WM) stores the information people are actively paying attention to, but it is limited in capacity and duration;
    - long-term memory (LTM) is almost limitless and contains the knowledge collected over a lifetime;
    - LTM is organized in schemas, which are massive groupings of information around a particular topic, such as everything one knows about airplanes;
    - learning occurs when information is repeated, practiced, or rehearsed enough times within WM to become part of LTM.
- Cognitive load theory (CLT) describes how instruction is influenced by the limitations and organization of WM and LTM:
  - there are three types of cognitive load:
    - intrinsic load is based on the inherent complexity of the material being taught;

- - o extraneous load is based on ineffective instructional exercises that increase cognitive load, distracting one from learning, regardless of the material being taught;
  - o germane load is based on instructional exercises that enhance learning rather than detract from it.
  - the goal of instructional designers is to balance these three forms of cognitive load without overloading the learner's WM.
- Constructivism is a learning theory that suggests that knowledge is inextricably tied to an individual's experiences:
  - the goal of instruction is to provide contexts and support to allow learners to relate new information to previous experiences.
- Expertise has a strong influence on the effectiveness of e-learning:
  - the expertise reversal effect describes how training that improves the skills of novices may provide no benefit to experts, or might even decrease their skills.
- Motivation is an important consideration in e-learning:
  - intrinsic motivation is based on the individual's natural interest or curiosity in a topic;
  - extrinsic motivation refers to external influences that drive an individual to learn;
  - interactive practice exercises, challenges, and games can be incorporated into e-learning to improve motivation.
- Aviation training has a history of instruction through an apprenticeship approach:
  - a weakness of apprenticeships is that learners are not able to observe expert thought processes and decision-making patterns;
  - a cognitive apprenticeship approach to training makes expert thought processes visible to learners, allowing the learners to incrementally improve their problem-solving skills.

Chapter 5

The Feasibility of e-Learning for Nontechnical Skills

Consistency is the last refuge of the unimaginative.

—Oscar Wilde

Overview

The purpose of this chapter is to:

- review the history and evolution of crew resource management (CRM) training;
- identify pertinent CRM issues, including content ambiguity, assessment issues, effective feedback, and transfer of training;
- introduce single-pilot resource management (SRM) training;
- explore the feasibility of computer-based CRM and SRM.

Introduction

Broadly, all aviation training can be broken down into two categories:

1. Technical aviation training—that is, traditional pilot training, both in the air and on the ground. This training, which focuses on the airmanship knowledge and skills required to attain a pilot's license or rating, is commonly referred to as 'hard-skill' instruction.
2. Nontechnical aviation training—which entails instruction of supplementary safety skills that are beyond the scope of traditional pilot training, such CRM. This training is commonly referred to as 'soft-skill' instruction.

Researchers have questioned whether e-learning is a feasible option for delivering nontechnical training (Derouin et al. 2005). Early work suggests that e-learning of soft skills can improve pilot performance, but much additional work is required to specifically identify which aspects of nontechnical training are well suited to e-learning, and which are not (Kearns, in press). The purpose of this chapter is to present the potential advantages of nontechnical e-learning, with the hope that future research will address the many unanswered questions in this area.

Crew Resource Management (CRM)

In the 1970s a series of aviation accidents occurred, in which flight crew errors were the causal factor (Flin, O'Connor and Mearns 2002). In an effort to address the causes of these accidents, the National Aeronautics and Space Administration (NASA) held a workshop for the air transport industry in 1979, titled 'Resource Management on the Flightdeck' (Helmreich, Merritt and Wilhelm 1999). Research presented at the workshop identified human error as the primary cause of most crashes, specifically decision making, leadership, and interpersonal communications between the captain and first officer. As a result of these presentations, Cockpit Resource Management (CRM) was developed as a program to train pilot teams in the effective use of these nontechnical skills.

Throughout the tenure of CRM training, significant advancements have been made in developing CRM concepts and understanding how they should be delivered. Therefore, reviewing the CRM literature identifies the opportunities and challenges faced in the design of nontechnical pilot training. Current challenges in CRM training include content ambiguity, appropriate assessment techniques, and maximizing positive transfer of training. It is important to understand these issues before embarking on the development of computer-based CRM.

History of Crew Resource Management (CRM)

CRM training has evolved significantly since its inception. Early CRM courses, which were developed and employed by United Airlines in North America and KLM in Europe, focused on diagnosing managerial styles (Flin, O'Connor and Mearns 2002; Helmreich, Merritt and Wilhelm 1999). CRM training was defined as 'the effective use of all resources (hardware, software and liveware) to achieve safe and efficient flight operations' (Jensen 1995: 116). The goal of this training was correcting deficiencies in behavior, such as overly authoritative behaviors on the part of captains. These courses encouraged effective interpersonal behavior without clearly defining what that meant on a flight deck, and often included non-aviation-related games to illustrate concepts. An effective spin-off of CRM training was Line Oriented Flight Training (LOFT), which allowed crews to practice CRM skills in a flight simulator. However, acceptance of these courses was poor among pilots, who commonly rejected early CRM training as 'charm school' (Helmreich, Merritt and Wilhelm 1999).

In 1986, the name of CRM training was changed from Cockpit Resource Management to Crew Resource Management, reflecting the change in emphasis toward group dynamics. CRM courses became more aviation focused and team oriented, concentrating on effective teamwork and flight safety skills. Acceptance of this generation of CRM increased, however there were still criticisms that the content was 'laced with psycho-babble' (Helmreich, Merritt and Wilhelm 1999: 21).

In the 1990s, CRM training began addressing more aviation-specific tasks, in addition to teamwork and safety. Technical training was integrated to focus on specific pilot skills such as programming flight deck automation. Training also began to address human factors issues (Helmreich, Merritt and Wilhelm 1999). Human factors skills are essential for effective interactions with systems. The teaching, evaluation, and learning of these skills are based on foundational theories within psychology, ergonomics, physiology, and engineering (Wickens et al. 2003). In addition, CRM training was expanded to include other airline employee groups such as flight attendants, dispatchers, and maintenance staff. These courses effectively broadened the scope of individuals who constitute a crew, but they also had the unexpected effect of overgeneralizing the focus of CRM at the expense of the main goal, which was reducing pilot error.

The premise of current CRM training, which focuses on error management, is that human error is inevitable and that CRM training provides a set of error countermeasures. Ideally, instruction should be focused on normalizing and managing error, through teaching human performance limitations (Helmreich, Merritt and Wilhelm 1999).

CRM is increasingly accepted as a crucial component of pilot training. An International Air Transport Association survey indicated that 96 percent of respondents, including all major international airlines, were actively running CRM courses. More than a decade ago, the Joint Aviation Authorities (JAA) in Europe established regulations requiring all pilots in multi-crew flight decks to complete CRM training (Flin, O'Connor and Mearns 2002). In the United States, CRM training became mandatory for military aviators in the early 1990s and for commercial flight crews in 1998 (Salas et al. 2006). Airlines invest millions of dollars in CRM training, and other industries (such as the medical, offshore oil, ATC, nuclear power, and maritime shipping industries) have followed suit (Flin, O'Connor and Mearns 2002; Salas et al. 2001). In a meta-analysis of 58 CRM evaluation studies, Salas et al. (2001) conclude that, 'CRM training programs seem to produce positive participant reactions, learning, and application of learned behavior via simulators, on line, or on the job' (671). CRM training is necessary in aviation, because human error is the result of natural human limitations when combined with complicated automated systems. CRM is one of the strategies an organization can use to control error (Helmreich, Merritt and Wilhelm 1999).

Pertinent Crew Resource Management (CRM) Issues

Although CRM is increasingly accepted by industry, the literature points to several areas that remain under investigation. It is important to note that there is a large body of CRM literature exploring team dynamics and teamwork principles (Salas, Burke and Cannon-Bowers 2000). However, the teamwork research component of CRM course content is beyond the scope of this chapter.

Content ambiguity   A primary goal of aviation safety researchers is to maximize safety by addressing or eliminating sources of human error. CRM training is an example of this pursuit. Unfortunately, there is significant ambiguity and confusion in the literature on how this training should be carried out. Some literature divides CRM concepts into two categories: cognitive skills, such as decision making and workload management; and social skills, such as leadership and team work (Flin and Martin 2001). Another group categorizes the goal of CRM training as developing safe and efficient attitudes toward teamwork, personality, and social interactions, while other researchers maintain that behavioral skills are paramount (Salas, Rhodenizer and Bowers 2000).

There is also significant ambiguity regarding appropriate instructional delivery methods. Unfortunately, in traditional lecture-based CRM training, students may not learn how and when to use the knowledge they have received. As a result, students may obtain declarative knowledge but not the procedural knowledge required for the training to transfer to real-world situations (Salas, Rhodenizer and Bowers 2000). A combination of lectures and active practice addresses this problem by allowing students to understand situations in which the knowledge should be applied. However, a standardized method of allowing for active practice remains elusive. Some courses utilize games and role playing, while others rely on high-fidelity simulations (Salas, Rhodenizer and Bowers 2000).

Behavioral modeling techniques provide yet another active practice approach. Behavioral modeling is a process in which students observe others demonstrating positive and negative models of behavior, internalize the information, and develop the motivation to apply the correct behaviors to their job (Salas, Rhodenizer and Bowers 2000).

Active practice is also accomplished through scenario-based training (SBT), which is typically conducted in a flight simulator (Helmreich, Merritt and Wilhelm 1999). One example of SBT is LOFT, in which a learning scenario is designed to target a specific component of CRM, such as communication, teamwork, or decision making (Salas, Rhodenizer and Bowers 2000).

CRM training is widely used, and there is great variation in the content and delivery of CRM training, even within the same airline, as instructors use different teaching strategies. Therefore it is a challenge to determine which approach is most effective. Before this issue can be ameliorated, a standardized CRM theory must be agreed upon and a standardized training curriculum must be developed and widely distributed.

Assessment issues   Assessing the quality of individual CRM programs and the overall impact of this training on the industry's safety record is a second topic of interest in the literature. Assessment challenges are mainly the result of wide variability and lack of standardization in CRM training. The literature tends to evaluate CRM programs according to their impact on behaviors and attitudes, learner reactions on course evaluations, and improvements to the industry's safety record.

CRM training programs can be assessed by evaluating behaviors and attitudes in the cockpit (Helmreich, Merritt and Wilhelm 1999). However, it is difficult to determine whether pilots are only employing CRM concepts because they are under assessment; in other words, the observed behavior might not reflect the pilots' real-world practices. Overall, the literature is divided on the impact of CRM on learning and behavior; a review of several sources indicated that CRM training produces positive learner reactions (Salas, Wilson and Burke 2006). In addition, crews indicate that this training is important and effective. Unfortunately, assessment has revealed that CRM training will not benefit everyone, as a small number of individuals (often referred to as 'cowboys' or 'boomerangs') will reject this training (Helmreich, Merritt and Wilhelm 1999).

Because CRM training has been in existence for more than 30 years, several researchers have attempted to assess its impact on the aviation industry. However, it is difficult to say whether CRM training has increased the safety of flight, because accident rates are so low and CRM programs so variable (Helmreich, Merritt and Wilhelm 1999). In fact, the number of accidents caused by a breakdown in CRM has been fairly consistent over the last 30 years (Salas, Wilson and Burke 2006).

Rather than utilizing a single means of evaluating the impact of CRM training, several studies implement Kirkpatrick's (1998) five-level typology, which assesses training on the basis of trainees' affective feelings about the utility of the program, the knowledge gained through the program, desired changes in behavior, knowledge transfer from training to job performance, and organizational impact. A recent literature review revealed that 43 percent of studies utilized this evaluation approach (Salas, Wilson and Burke 2006). Kirkpatrick's five levels of evaluation are discussed in more detail in Chapter 12.

A study of the effectiveness of CRM training concluded that researchers should conduct evaluations that are sound, systematic, reliable, and conducted at multiple levels. In addition, if the bottom-line impacts of CRM on aviation safety are to be determined, safety measures other than accident rates must be explored (Salas, Wilson and Burke 2006). Finally, Flin and Martin (2001) suggest that regulating bodies should develop ways of assessing nontechnical CRM skills of individual pilots. Such assessments would be included as part of a pilot licensing flight examination and would allow for further integration of CRM concepts into mainstream pilot training and evaluation.

Effective feedback Another issue under investigation is how to provide learners with effective feedback regarding their CRM skills following training. Feedback is a powerful tool that can be utilized to enhance learning. Within CRM training, feedback addressing group processes is a challenge, as a correct decision in the cockpit does not necessarily indicate that an effective team process was employed (Salas, Rhodenizer and Bowers 2000). As Salas and colleagues explain, even if a copilot was reluctant to share information about deteriorating weather conditions that could impact a landing decision, it is possible for a safe landing to be made. Therefore, safe and correct performance does not directly indicate that effective nontechnical skills were utilized. Additional research defining optimal feedback strategies is required.

Transfer of training   Transfer of training refers to how well learning in one environment, such as a simulator or classroom, improves performance in another environment, such as in an aircraft (Wickens et al. 2003). The goal of any training is to produce positive transfer to the operational environment. In the case of CRM, positive transfer would be evidenced by pilots adopting appropriate attitudes, behaviors, and social interactions post-training. Positive transfer of CRM skills to the operational environment has been documented by several investigations (Beard, Salas and Prince 1995; Salas, Wilson and Burke 2006). A significant factor in positive transfer is supervisor support for CRM training and an organizational climate of acceptance of CRM concepts (Salas, Rhodenizer and Bowers 2000). Such support and acceptance are crucial, because the training loses operational validity if CRM concepts are not evaluated and demonstrated by check airmen and if pilots do not sense management's support. A disturbing finding is that acceptance of CRM concepts degrades over time, even after recurrent training. It is believed that a lack of managerial support is at least partially responsible for this degradation (Helmreich, Merritt and Wilhelm 1999). Therefore, for CRM to be widely adopted in an organization, it is crucial for management in the upper echelons to support CRM techniques and to integrate these concepts into operational procedures and checklists.

Computer-Based Nontechnical Pilot Training

Even though the tragic terrorist attacks of September 11, 2001 nearly bankrupted the airline industry, the number of new pilot jobs is expected to grow at least 40 percent over the next decade, and the volume of air traffic in the United States is expected to triple by 2020 (Federal Aviation Administration 2007; Raisinghani et al. 2005). In addition, the general pilot population is aging, and a significant number of replacement pilots will be required to cover retirements. Therefore, the industry's training needs are expected to increase in volume as well as complexity, as pilots will be operating in densely populated airspace (Raisinghani et al. 2005). As a result, the industry needs to continually focus resources on investigating innovative teaching practices and emerging instructional technologies.

Despite the need for nontechnical training that is effective, standardized, widely distributable, and affordable, computer-based CRM training has received minimal attention (Brannick, Prince and Salas 2005). A general opinion in the industry is that CRM training is ill suited to computer-based learning (CBL), not only because of the team focus of CRM, but also because of the active practice requirement, which is typically conducted in a simulator. In addition, research has yet to determine which CRM delivery methods—asynchronous, synchronous, or blended learning—would be most suitable for pilot training.

Ideally, instructional materials should support auditory, visual, and tactile learners. However, traditional nontechnical instruction is delivered in a lecture format with visual aids. This training method best supports auditory and visual learners. The problem is that 44 percent of pilots are tactile learners (Raisinghani et al. 2005). Delivering nontechnical content in an online environment would allow for the design of interactive materials that better support pilot learning.

Although to date there appears to be no research evaluating a fully online and comprehensive CRM training course, significant research has been performed on the use of inexpensive personal computer (PC) based simulations and games for crew training. Several PC-based flight simulation programs that are on the market allow pilots to refine their skills (Koonce and Bramble 1998). There are also games that offer a variety of aircraft, the ability to fly out of virtually any major airport, weather controls that reduce ceilings and visibility, and the capability to fail certain systems or instruments for practice purposes. With the addition of reasonably priced yoke, throttle lever, or rudder pedals, some low-fidelity simulations have the potential to become more than just a game. This reasonably priced alternative to high-fidelity flight simulators would allow students to complete the active practice component of CRM training from a PC.

Simulators provide a common method of evaluating transfer of training of CRM concepts in aviation operations. In practice, many organizations and CRM instructors are of the opinion that high-fidelity simulators are ideal for learning. High-fidelity simulations are characterized by high-scene detail and motion platforms. However, investigations have shown no differences in training transfer between high- and low-fidelity simulations (Salas, Bowers and Rhodenizer 1998). Research suggests that low-fidelity simulation is effective as long as it simulates the cognitive processes required in the real world; this principle is known as *psychological fidelity* (Bowers and Jentsch 2001). Such findings have led to the conclusion that high fidelity is not a requirement for effective training and transfer (Baker et al. 1993; Koonce and Bramble 1998; Salas, Bowers and Rhodenizer 1998). In addition, Jentsch and Bowers (1998) conclude that aviators find low-fidelity simulations realistic and acceptable for nontechnical training.

Brannick, Prince and Salas (2005) conducted an investigation into the transfer of training of a nontechnical piloting skill taught with a PC-based simulator. The study specifically targeted pilot assertiveness by encouraging junior pilots to point out errors to senior pilots, because a lack of junior pilot assertiveness has been the causal factor in several aviation accidents. Brannick and colleagues evaluated the quasi-transfer of skills from a PC-based simulator to a high-fidelity simulator rather than from the PC-based simulator to the operational environment. Although Helmreich, Merritt and Wilhelm (1999) argue that this is a less appropriate evaluation method, it is more practical financially and logistically. Brannick, Prince and Salas found positive quasi-transfer from a PC-based simulator to a high-fidelity simulator, providing strong evidence that inexpensive simulators can effectively teach nontechnical skills. Further research is required to determine whether positive results can be produced for other nontechnical skills, including communication, situation awareness, workload management, and decision making (Brannick, Prince and Salas 2005).

Like pilots, aircraft maintenance technicians (AMTs) pilots, must employ nontechnical skills such as coordination, communication, and cooperation in order to perform their tasks effectively. Kraus et al. (1997) found no performance differences between AMT students who completed computer-based vs. traditional lecture-based nontechnical training, and in fact CBT was superior in terms of standardization, geographic and temporal adaptability, record keeping, cost effectiveness, and access to a multitude of situations and aircraft.

Single-Pilot Resource Management (SRM)

Notably lacking in the literature is the application of CRM training to the single-pilot general aviation (GA) sector. GA includes all flights not associated with airline or military activity. In recent years, with the introduction of glass cockpit avionic displays, GA aircraft have experienced a rapid increase in technological sophistication. In addition, very light jets (VLJs) are set to revolutionize GA and the aviation industry as a whole. VLJs provide the speed and efficiency of jet-powered flight to moderately experienced pilots at a reasonable cost of ownership (Strait 2006). As a result, GA pilots are flying faster and more technologically advanced aircraft than were previously available.

Trollip and Jensen (1991) have determined that pilots with limited experience are particularly susceptible to accidents and incidents, as their confidence level exceeds their level of skill. In particular, two periods are especially dangerous: (1) at approximately 100 hours total time, when pilots have accumulated about 50 hours past their private pilot license; and (2) between 50 and 100 hours after completing their instrument rating. Typically, both of these high-risk periods will take place while a pilot is operating in the GA sector. Therefore, it's important to provide nontechnical safety training to the GA pilot demographic.

The industry has recognized the need for CRM concepts to be taught in GA to single-pilot operators. A single-pilot resource management (SRM) training overview has been developed (FITS n.d.; NBAA Safety Committee 2005); however, SRM training is in its infancy, and this term is not well known or documented in the academic literature. According to the descriptions formulated by the Federal Aviation Administration (FAA) and NBAA, SRM consists of nontechnical training, and its goal is to reduce pilot error. The major distinction between SRM and CRM is that aircrew coordination and communication, which are major components of CRM training, are not included in SRM. However, other CRM components are adapted for single pilot operations and included in SRM. These include decision making, situation awareness, workload management, resource management, automation management, and information management (FITS n.d., NBAA Safety Committee 2005). All of these factors are important to pilot safety.

Impact of Computer-Based Crew Resource Management (CRM) or Single-Pilot Resource Management (SRM)

Content Ambiguity

As a preliminary training program, a well-designed e-learning course could set the benchmark for SRM training and avoid much of the content ambiguity that exists within the CRM literature. Further research could be based on best practices identified in the CRM literature, and would refine the content and delivery of a nontechnical e-learning course until the best combination of cognitive, social, attitudinal, and behavioral instruction were determined. Once this refinement was accomplished, the online nature of the course would allow for its unlimited distribution, which in turn could support the foundation of a standardized curriculum.

Research suggests that integration of a PC-based flight simulator into e-learning is a feasible and effective option for active practice (Koonce and Bramble 1998). An additional option is mental practice. As all participants in SRM training would be licensed pilots, it would be possible to include imagination exercises as a form of active practice (Wiley and Voss 1999). Doing so would eliminate complications associated with delivering yoke, throttle, and rudder pedals and would also reduce the cost of the software. Overall, an e-learning course would be a powerful step toward ameliorating the content ambiguity that plagues CRM, and avoiding it altogether with SRM.

Assessment Issues

Accident rates in the airline industry are low, and CRM programs are widely variable. Thus a major obstacle to the acceptance of CRM training is the difficulty of clearly determining the impact of CRM (Helmreich, Merritt and Wilhelm 1999). It would be unrealistic to claim that developing an e-learning course would create a statistically significant improvement in the industry's safety record, as only a small percentage of the industry is likely to complete such training. However, an e-learning program offers some advantages, including the ability to automatically track learner performance to (1) measure the decay in performance benefits over time and (2) compare learners' accident rates to the industry standard.

Upon creation of a complete e-learning program, it is crucial that the Kirkpatrick-based (1998) five-level typology assessment presented by Salas, Wilson and Burke (2006) be utilized. Doing so will ensure that the program's assessment is systematic and reliable and that it allows for effectively targeted improvements. Future research is required to identify the affective, knowledge, behavioral changes, and organizational impact of SRM training.

Feedback

e-Learning presents novel opportunities to provide feedback. It is possible to establish a synchronous connection in which an instructor observes a student's simulation flight. This would allow for a post-flight debriefing—which is standard practice in traditional pilot training—through instant messaging or computer-mediated video conferencing.

e-Learning also presents another feedback option: automated computer-generated data. Computer feedback has some advantages over instructor feedback, including the ability to be completely objective and to produce a hard- or soft-copy performance record (Koonce and Bramble 1998). Automated computer-generated data can be a valuable training aid, as it is a standardized means for students to compare performance against previous sessions.

Transfer of Training

For computer-based SRM training to be effective, positive transfer to the operational environment is crucial. Several strategies can be utilized by an instructional designer to support this concept. Such strategies include incorporating sound instructional practices, ensuring an appropriate and effective curriculum, designing organizational and managerial support, and allowing for a means of active practice. However, there is no way of guaranteeing that positive transfer will occur. Therefore, transfer of training from a computer-based training program to the real world or a simulator should be assessed post-training.

Conclusion

Overall, it is clear that computer-based nontechnical pilot training offers clear advantages. Not only is this training cost effective and convenient, but it may ameliorate several of the issues that currently exist within CRM training, including content ambiguity, assessment, feedback, and transfer of training.

Practical Summary

- Broadly, all aviation training falls into one of two categories:
    - technical training, also called hard-skill instruction, which teaches the knowledge and skills required to fly a plane;
    - nontechnical training, also called soft-skill instruction, which teaches supplementary safety skills.
- Crew resource management (CRM), which was created in 1979, is the best-known example of nontechnical training.

- Although CRM has been in existence for more than 30 years, it is plagued with some unresolved problems, which include:
    - *Content ambiguity.* Large variations in content and delivery exist in CRM training across organizations and sometimes within organizations, as each instructor has a different style and focus.
    - *Assessment.* Although CRM is accepted as important training, it is unclear exactly what impact CRM has on individual performance or on industry accident rates.
    - *Feedback.* Feedback is a powerful tool to enhance learning. However, it is a challenge to incorporate feedback into CRM training, because a correct action by a flight crew does not necessarily indicate that an effective team process was used.
    - *Transfer of training.* Although CRM skills seem to transfer to the operational environment, acceptance of CRM concepts tends to degrade over time. It is believed that increased managerial support may reduce this degradation.
- Single-pilot resource management (SRM), a training program that is still in its infancy, focuses on applying CRM concepts to single-pilot operations.
- e-Learning, as a training delivery option, may ameliorate the unresolved CRM problems and help avoid these problems altogether within SRM training.

Chapter 6
Incorporating Practice into e-Learning

Tell me and I forget.
Teach me and I remember.
Involve me and I learn.

—Benjamin Franklin

Overview

The purpose of this chapter is to:

- present the five principles of effective e-learning practice;
- describe how games and simulation can be designed to support e-learning practice;
- review two options for incorporating simulation practice into e-learning: low-fidelity simulation and guided mental practice (GMP);
- review the background theories and the effectiveness of GMP.

Incorporating Practice into e-Learning in Aviation

It is not the intention of this chapter to suggest that computer-based practice scenarios could replace the in-aircraft training required for a student pilot to gain the skills, knowledge, and attitudes of a professional pilot. Rather, an opportunity exists for e-learning to support ground school through the integration of realistic flight scenarios and activities that allow students the opportunity to practice applying classroom concepts to real-world situations from the comfort of their computer. In this manner, e-learning can enhance current practices without sacrificing the instructional expertise that exists within the industry.

There is typically a complete lack of practice within the ground school component of pilot training. Pilots who do not have practice opportunities can possess declarative knowledge but lack the procedural knowledge required to apply the skills to real-world operations. Implementing a combination of lecture and active practice addresses this problem by allowing students to understand and recognize situations in which the knowledge should be applied (Salas, Rhodenizer and Bowers 2000). Research has demonstrated that when active practice is included in instruction it enhances both psychomotor and cognitive performance—two crucial components of pilot training (Rosenbaum, Carlson and

Gilmore 2001). Although e-learning provides several advantages, the ability to incorporate an effective method of practice into aviation training is a challenge that must be addressed.

The Five Practice Principles

Practice is a crucially important aspect of any training program. Within e-learning, the term *interaction* is used interchangeably with practice, to describe any element of a training program that solicits a response from learners. The following five principles will help course designers and instructors develop effective e-learning practice exercises (Clark and Mayer 2008):

1. Practice should be designed to target specific performance gaps:
   - Practice should be presented in a context that represents the real-world work environment where the skill will be used. To target the problems the training is meant to solve, the practice design should be based on a task analysis. Practice based on memorization and regurgitation of concepts should be avoided, as these abilities do not reflect a true understanding of the concept (Clark and Mayer 2008).
2. Practice should include explanatory feedback:
   - Feedback is a powerful learning tool, as it provides immediate knowledge of results, which learners can use to modify incorrect actions or ideas. Rather than just stating whether the learner's response is correct or incorrect, it is recommended that instructors inform the learner of the reasoning behind the correct answer (Clark and Mayer 2008).
3. The amount of e-learning practice should be tailored to job requirements:
   - Although it is widely accepted that practice improves learning, integration of practice should be carefully thought out. Practice exercises are expensive and time consuming to create, and also time consuming for learners to complete. In addition, the benefits of practice diminish quickly, with large performance gains associated with early practice, and small gains associated with subsequent practice (Rosenbaum, Carlson and Gilmore 2001). It is also known that practice that is spaced out throughout the course of learning leads to better retention over time (Clark and Mayer 2008). Lastly, if the job requires learners to respond to events quickly with error-free performance, a large amount of practice is required to allow learners to respond to events automatically. This ability to respond to events quickly and accurately is called *automaticity*. e-Learning allows for timing and analysis of learner responses to determine when learners begin to develop automaticity (Clark and Mayer 2008).

4. Practice should be developed with an understanding of how and when to use multimedia:
   - The design considerations of e-learning practice exercises differ from those for the rest of the instruction program. On-screen text is a preferable option for practice instructions and feedback, as it allows learners time to think about exercises. Audio should be avoided, as it is too transient. In addition, the graphic design should clearly distinguish question, answer, and feedback sections of the screen. However, these three sections should be as close together as possible to allow students to reference the question, remember their response, and compare it against the corrective feedback. Lastly, practice exercises should be designed free of distracting animations, music, or stories (Clark and Mayer 2008).
5. e-Learning should transition gradually from examples to practice exercises:
   - Although practice is important, it is also a cognitively demanding task that can easily overwhelm novice learners. Therefore, Clark and Mayer (2008) suggest faded worked examples. Faded worked examples begin with a practice scenario presented to the learner, in which the e-learning program describes all of the steps required for successful task performance and then presents questions to test understanding. Next, another scenario is presented, with only portions of the steps completed by the e-learning program; learners are asked to provide the missing information. This process eventually builds to the level where learners are able to complete the entire scenario independently (Clark and Mayer 2008).

The types of practice activities that can be integrated into e-learning are limited only by the designer's imagination. Popular types of interactions in e-learning include the following (adapted from Horton 2006):

- Activities that require the learner to mentally process information; these usually do not involve physical actions:
  - *Virtual field trips*. Virtual field trips present videos of historically relevant locations such as the sand dunes of Kitty Hawk, North Carolina, or professionally relevant locations such as the floor of an international airport.
  - *Electronic readings*. These are text-based documents for learners to read on-screen or to print out.
  - *Storytelling*. An instructor (either a live instructor who is connected synchronously with the students, or an automated instructor such as an animated coach character) tells a story about a personal experience that is relevant to the instructional content. Stories are a very natural way to learn, as this is the way that mankind has historically conveyed information.

- *Presentation.* A grouping of organized content is displayed via PowerPoint, video, or podcast.
- Activities that require self-explanation or self-organization by the learner:
  - *Job aids.* These are electronic tools that provide learners with the opportunity to use their new knowledge to solve real-world problems; for example, a virtual aircraft that a flight student can interact with to practice walk-around techniques (checking fuel, flight surfaces, and so on).
  - *Thinking activities.* Rather than having learners memorize new concepts, these activities require them to think deeply about an issue, apply it to other domains, analyze it for potential problems, and brainstorm other options. For example, once students have the knowledge and understanding of a super-jumbo jet (such as the Airbus 380), they would be asked to brainstorm the advantages and disadvantages of this type of aircraft for different aviation groups (such as airport management, airlines, pilots, passengers, and ground crew).
  - *Independent research.* Learners are given an issue and required to search through various sources (such as electronic textbooks or the Internet) to find more information about the issue and form an opinion in favor of or against a proposed solution.
- Activities that require action from learners:
  - *Interactions.* Activities that allow learners to practice applying knowledge, skills, and attitudes may include group-based activities, simple drill-and-practice exercises to automate skills, or electronic tools that a learner must use to interact with or fix an object.
  - *Discovery activities.* Discovery activities allow learners to explore and experiment with an electronic medium. Rather than presenting learners with the answer, this process provides guidance so that learners can discover the answer independently. Examples include case studies describing a real-world problem, role-play presenting realistic cockpit dynamics, and virtual wind tunnels to explore aerodynamics.
  - *Games and simulations.* These are explored in the following section.

Games and Simulations

Games

Although video games are often regarded as toys, they can be a powerful learning tool that is fun and therefore improves extrinsic motivation. The best video games incorporate many of the same principles that are used in effective teaching, including feedback, interactivity, challenges of increasing difficulty, and multimodal presentation (Horton 2002). Research suggests that some games, such as PC-based flight simulators, are suitable for pilot nontechnical training (Jentsch and Bowers 1998).

Horton (2002) explains that games are advantageous because of their ability to:

- engage learners who find classroom and e-learning courses boring;
- motivate voluntary learners to take a test;
- promote discovery learning, allowing learners to identify and analyze important situations themselves;
- demonstrate consequences, as the only good time to crash an aircraft is within a flight simulator;
- promote extensive practice (Horton 2002).

However, games are not well suited for all people or learning objectives. The negative aspects of learning games include:

- poor ability to teach a large amount of high-detail factual data;
- inability to make boring subject matter interesting;
- inability to replace traditional education tools, including books, instructors, and traditional classroom and e-learning methods (Horton 2002).

Overall, games are an excellent way of engaging modern learners who are 'digital natives.' No longer are computer games just for children, as computer or video games are played in 68 percent of American households and the average game player age is 35. In fact, 25 percent of gamers are over the age of 50 (Entertainment Software Association 2009).

Simulations

Broadly, there are two options available to simulate the in-flight environment for e-learning practice scenarios: low-fidelity flight simulators, and mental practice.

Most airlines utilize high-fidelity flight simulators for practice. High-fidelity simulators are expensive devices (often costing millions of dollars) that accurately replicate cockpit instrumentation and in-flight visuals, motion, and sounds. By comparison, low-fidelity simulators are PC-based games that are very affordable (approximately 50 USD). One of the best known low-fidelity simulators is Microsoft Flight Simulator.

Investigations have shown no differences in training transfer between high- and low-fidelity simulators (Brannick, Prince and Salas 2005; Koonce and Bramble 1998; Salas, Bowers and Rhodenizer 1998). The low-fidelity aspect does not necessarily present a problem, as 'the best simulation in the world does not guarantee learning' (Salas, Bowers and Rhodenizer 1998: 200). Research suggests that low-fidelity simulation is effective as long as it facilitates the cognitive processes required in the real world; this correspondence is called *psychological fidelity* (Bowers and Jentsch 2001). Incorporating low-fidelity interactive simulation into aviation e-learning would allow developers to create realistic in-flight scenarios for practice.

Several PC-based low-fidelity flight simulator games, which incorporate peripheral yoke, throttle, and rudder pedals, are marketed as a means for pilots to refine their skills. These games are a feasible option within an organization's computer lab, where peripheral devices can be made available to learners. However, wide distribution of e-learning that incorporates this method of practice is complicated by the high bandwidth requirements and the cost of flight control peripherals. Therefore, it is important to consider a less obvious practice option for delivering effective e-learning: mental practice—and specifically a new concept known as *guided mental practice* (GMP).

Mental practice, which is typically an entirely internal process devoid of visual references, is accomplished through visualizing or imagining a flight situation or scenario. GMP differs from traditional mental practice, in that GMP makes use of an e-learning program that guides the learner through the practice exercise. GMP is facilitated by a video of a computer-based flight scenario embedded within an e-learning program but does not involve any hands-on interaction. In GMP, learners are asked to view the flight scenario video and imagine themselves as the pilot of the flight. Early research suggests that learners who complete training with GMP demonstrate the same improvements in situation awareness as those who complete training with a low-fidelity interactive flight simulator for practice (Kearns, in press).

Before we review the methods of incorporating GMP into e-learning, it is necessary to understand expert performance research and cognitive load theory (CLT), which provide the theoretical underpinnings for complex skill instruction. Expert performance research investigates how experts have gained skills historically. This focus provides an understanding of the mechanisms behind the superior performance of experts; however, translating these mechanisms into instructional recommendations is not a priority in expert performance research (van Gog et al. 2005). CLT, on the other hand, focuses on the instructional strategies that support skill acquisition in learning settings, and is based on an understanding of how humans process information.

Expert performance research   Expert performance research is described in Chapter 4. For the purpose of understanding GMP, keep in mind that expert performance is related to the amount of deliberate practice extended by the learner (van Gog et al. 2005). Typically, the kind of active practice that is included in nontechnical training programs focuses on developing conditioned responses rather than on developing higher order thinking skills (Robertson 2005). In pilot training, however, emphasis should be placed on designing scenarios as deliberate practice activities that promote high-order thinking skills rather than rote memorization.

Cognitive Load Theory (CLT) A discussion of CLT, including an overview of working memory (WM), long-term memory (LTM), and schema development, is presented in Chapter 4. Regarding mental practice, CLT suggests that the process of imagining helps learners organize new material into schemas, and that this organization in turn increases a learner's speed and accuracy in using new information in the real-world environment (Leahy and Sweller 2005). CLT is internationally recognized and has been empirically validated in several studies (Bannert 2002). Various investigations have indicated that instructional strategies based on CLT, such as mental practice, facilitate novice learning but are less effective with increasing learner expertise. This phenomenon is termed the *expertise reversal effect* (Driskell, Copper and Moran 1994). However, it has not been conclusively determined that CLT-based instructional formats do not work for learners with high expertise. Still, this research motivates investigators to question not only how to design instruction for learners who have progressed beyond the first levels of mastery, but also how expertise is acquired and what fosters this acquisition (van Gog et al. 2005).

Guided Mental Practice (GMP)

Leahy and Sweller (2004) explain that mental practice is a form of deliberate practice, as the goal of both is to 'process material through working memory with the intention of strengthening schemas held in long-term memory' (859). Wiley and Voss (1999) determined that the kind of practice exercise is not important; what matters is that the practice exercises facilitate mental processes that lead to enhanced learning. Similarly, Jackson et al. (2001) state that 'humans have the ability to generate mental correlates of perceptual and motor events without any triggering external stimulus, a function known as imagery' (1133). This imagery, or mental practice, is a powerful instructional tool for improving performance on both cognitive and psychomotor skills (Driskell, Copper and Moran 1994). In fact, learners who imagine a concept or procedure often outperform those who study or practice it (Cooper et al. 2001; Leahy and Sweller 2004, 2005).

Mental practice is characterized by deliberately verbalizing or visualizing the information while imagining the concept (Leahy and Sweller 2005). Studies on the effect of mental practice come from various disciplines, including sport psychology, cognitive neuroscience, and cognitive psychology (Jackson et al. 2001). The instructional strategy of imagining to enhance learning and performance has a long history in the research literature, although the terminology varies. The terms *symbolic rehearsal* and *imaginary practice* originated in the 1930s (Perry 1939; Sackett 1934). Since that time, the terms *mental practice, introspective rehearsal, conceptualization, covert rehearsal,* and *mental rehearsal* have been used to describe the same phenomenon (Driskell, Copper and Moran 1994; Leahy and Sweller 2004). Although several studies have evaluated this phenomenon, some with inconclusive results, most indicate that mental practice does improve performance (Druckman and Swets 1988).

There are psychological and physiological similarities between movements that are physically executed and those that are imagined (Fadiga et al. 1999; Leonardo et al. 1995). Therefore, mental practice improvements are not limited to cognitive tasks but apply to performance on psychomotor tasks as well (Driskell, Copper and Moran 1994).

Many studies in the sport psychology discipline advocate mental practice as a method of enhancing motor skill performance, which in turn results in improved athletic skills (Driskell, Copper and Moran 1994; Feltz and Landers 1983; Maring, 1990). Surprisingly, investigations in this domain have even revealed gains in isometric muscle strength following mental practice (Cornwall, Bruscato and Barry 1991; Yue and Cole 1992). Although this result may seem like science fiction, these gains are documented as true and are attributed to the changes in the programming and planning processes of the motor system (Yue and Cole 1992).

Mental practice theories   Sackett's (1934) symbolic learning theory suggests that mental practice improves motor performance through a cognitive rehearsal of task components. This theory is consistent with the findings of several experiments, which indicated that mental practice was more effective for cognitively demanding tasks than for simple tasks (Driskell, Copper and Moran 1994). However, it does not explain the increase in muscle strength after mental practice (Yue and Cole 1992).

Paivio (1985) proposed another theory of mental practice. According to Paivio, performance improvements resulting from mental practice result from both cognitive and motivational aspects of an activity at several levels.

According to a third theory, the benefits associated with mental practice are similar to the benefits associated with self-explanation. Self-explanation research has found that individuals who effectively problem-solve are likely to explain the material to themselves (Renkl 1999; Wong, Lawson and Keeves 2002). Cooper et al. (2001) maintained that this phenomenon is an example of mental practice occurring naturally. Self-explanation can be considered a form of deliberate practice that enhances the development of schemas (Ericsson and Charness 1994).

Mental practice literature   In their meta-analysis of mental practice experiments, Driskell, Copper and Moran (1994) formulated several important conclusions:

1. Although mental practice enhances performance for both cognitive and physical activities, the effect is stronger on cognitively complex tasks.
2. The benefits of mental practice decrease with longer intervals between practice and performance, decreasing by half after 14 days.
3. Mental practice is more beneficial for experienced subjects than for novices.
4. The number of mental practice trials does not impact performance.

5. As the length of mental practice increases, the performance benefits become smaller; a guideline of approximately 20 minutes for an overall training period is suggested.
6. No-significant-differences exist between effect sizes for no-contact groups and groups that performed a similar activity for an equivalent amount of time (Driskell, Copper and Moran 1994).

Cooper et al. (2001) support and expand upon Driskell, Copper and Moran's (1994) third claim by stating that the extent to which imagination can facilitate learning is related to the individual's existing schemas. This is a logical assertion, because if the learner lacks the foundational knowledge regarding how to conduct a particular activity, imagination learning is likely to cause cognitive overload due to WM limitations. However, for learners with experience in the domain, mental practice substantially facilitates learning (Cooper et al. 2001). This instructional effect is another example of expertise reversal, as it causes novices to fail where experts succeed (Kalyuga et al. 2003).

Pascual-Leone and colleagues (1995) evaluated the impact of mental practice on a one-handed, five-finger piano exercise. Within the study, a mental practice group and a physical practice group practiced piano exercises independently for two hours a day for five days. Over the five-day period, the mental practice group experienced significant performance improvements, although this improvement was significantly less than that associated with physical practice. After five days of mental practice, participants demonstrated the same level of performance as those who completed three days of physical practice. However, participants who completed five days of mental practice plus one physical practice session were able to reach the same level of performance as participants who completed five days of physical practice. Therefore, mental practice 'not only results in marked performance improvement but also seems to place the subjects at an advantage for further skill learning with minimal physical practice' (Pascual-Leone et al. 1995: 1037). This result has led researchers to combine physical and mental practice to produce a synergistic effect, improving performance beyond either effect alone (Jackson et al. 2001; McBride and Rothstein 1979).

The conclusion that mental practice enhances performance to a lesser degree than physical practice is not universally supported. A recent investigation found that mental practice created and maintained a level of performance that was comparable to physical practice on a typing task (Wohldmann, Healy and Bourne 2007).

Although significant evidence suggests its effectiveness, there is still variance of opinion regarding mental practice. The controversy mostly revolves around ambiguity regarding the ideal amount of practice, the ideal nature of a mental practice task, and the learner's expertise level (Hall, Buckolz and Fishburne 1992).

Mental Practice in Education and Training   There is little published literature on mental practice investigations in the educational domain, whether in training or higher education. Computer-assisted mental practice is also rarely addressed in the academic literature. However, a recent investigation developed a virtual reality system to guide a stroke victim through mental practice exercises in which a virtual reconstruction of arm movement was presented. The investigation determined that the device and associated mental practice resulted in significant improvements in arm movement. The study also concluded that technology-supported mental practice within training programs, such as GMP, are feasible and potentially effective means of improving motor skills (Gaggioli et al. 2006).

Conclusion

It is clear that practice is an important component of effective e-learning. The types of practice activities that can be developed are almost limitless. However, two types of practice are increasingly popular among e-learning designers and learners: games and simulations. This chapter considered two main options for the development of simulated practice scenarios: interactive low-fidelity simulation; and GMP, in which a pilot is presented with a video of a flight scenario and asked to imagine himself or herself as the pilot of the aircraft. The literature suggests that low-fidelity simulation is acceptable to pilots and an effective method of incorporating practice into e-learning. Alternatively, mental practice can improve both cognitive and psychomotor performance, although the e-learning instructional design community has yet to capitalize on this potential. Overall, effective practice activities have the potential to expand the capabilities of e-learning to enhance complex and highly technical skills.

Practical Summary

- It is unlikely that e-learning could ever replace in-aircraft flight training, although it can supplement ground school, which typically lacks any practice opportunities.
- Practice, also called *interaction* within e-learning, refers to any elements of training that solicit a response from learners.
- There are five e-learning practice principles. e-Learning practice exercises should:
  1. target performance gaps;
  2. include explanatory feedback;
  3. tailor the amount of practice to job requirements;
  4. incorporate multimedia thoughtfully;
  5. transition gradually from examples to practice exercises (adapted from Clark and Mayer 2008).

- The types of e-learning practice activities are limited only by one's imagination, but two popular types are games and simulations.
- Games, often regarded as toys, can be powerful learning tools that increase extrinsic motivation:
    - no longer are games just for children, as computer or video games are played in 68 percent of American households, and the average gamer age is 35!
- Incorporating simulations into e-learning is another practice option, accomplished through low-fidelity flight simulators or guided mental practice (GMP).
    - perhaps the best known PC-based low-fidelity simulator is Microsoft Flight Simulator:
        o research has shown no differences in training transfer between high- and low-fidelity simulations.
- In GMP, learners are presented with a video of a flight scenario and asked to imagine themselves as the pilot of the flight:
    - research has shown that this mental practice can improve both cognitive and psychomotor performance;
    - GMP is a cost-effective method of incorporating practice into e-learning.

PART II
Instructional Design for e-Learning in Aviation

Chapter 7
Instructional Design for e-Learning

It is a mistake to try to look too far ahead.
The chain of destiny can only be grasped one link at a time.

—Sir Winston Churchill

Overview

The purpose of this chapter is to introduce the instructional design process, through:

- Reviewing the ADDIE Model:
  - Analyze
  - Design
  - Develop
  - Implement
  - Evaluate.

Introduction

Most aviation companies would agree that training is expensive. There are direct costs of training, including instructor salaries, simulators, classrooms, and loss of productivity when pilots are pulled off-the-line. There are also indirect costs of *poor* training, such as mistakes that result in decreased productivity and delayed flights. Overall, it is crucial to deliver training that is tailored specifically to what people need to know and that also doesn't waste time with unnecessary information. In addition, the training must be consistent and delivered effectively. Instructional design is a tool that can be used to accomplish these goals.

Instructional design (ID), also referred to as instructional system design (ISD), is a systematic process of analyzing the need for instruction, designing effective content, developing training based upon sound instructional principles, implementing instruction by delivering it to learners, and evaluating the effect of the instruction. The systematic use of ID for the creation of e-learning increases the overall effectiveness of training (Salas et al. 2002).

Just as the modern approach to aviation safety has adopted a systems perspective, ID for e-learning applies a systems approach to training. This is the reason that the word *system* is included in the term *instructional system design*. Although the creation of a new course must always begin with an analysis, the systems perspective means that all aspects of the ID process are interactive and iterative (meaning they repeat). Often this repetition takes the form of redesigning a portion of training after evaluation has revealed some shortcomings. Once the need for revision is identified, the entire ID process cycles again, beginning with a new analysis and followed by design modification, the development of a revised course, implementation of the new course, and ultimately another evaluation. According to the ISD perspective, a systematic design process allows the development of instruction that is more effective, relevant, and efficient than the product of less rigorous approaches (Gustafson and Branch 1997)

Although many ID models exist, they all contain five basic elements: analysis, design, development, implementation, and evaluation (ADDIE). The original author of the ADDIE concept is unknown; however, this process has become synonymous with ID (Molenda 2003). ADDIE is not a complete model but rather a broad overview that provides guidance on what should be included in the ID process. Although the ADDIE acronym is sequential, it is actually an iterative process better represented by a circle than by a straight line. In other words, the evaluation portion of the process often identifies areas of the analysis, design, development, or implementation that must be reworked. Thus the process starts over, as any problems that have been identified must flow through the ADDIE process once again. This process is represented in Figure 7.1.

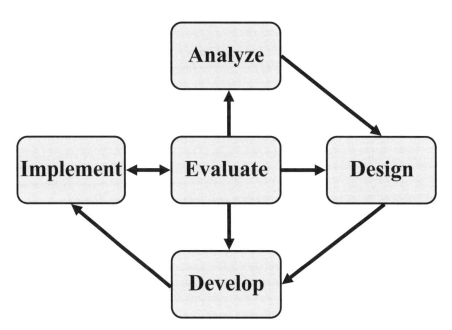

Figure 7.1 The ADDIE model of instructional design

Although the ADDIE model is an umbrella term that does not offer specific ID guidance, it is a convenient and memorable framework within which specific details can be organized. This part of the book offers detailed guidance on ID for e-learning, organized within the ADDIE framework. This chapter provides a brief introduction to instructional analysis, design, development, implementation, and evaluation for e-learning in aviation. The next five chapters describe these elements in detail.

Analysis

The ID process for e-learning is very similar to that of traditional classroom instruction. In fact, the entire analysis phase is identical for both face-to-face (F2F) and online instruction. However, the steps in the analysis phase for e-learning should be conducted with more rigor than ID for classroom instruction. The purpose of the analysis phase is to tailor instruction to the needs of the learners and the organization. Therefore, overall course effectiveness is highly dependent upon the analysis. In classroom instruction, a training activity that is not effective—perhaps because it is too simplistic for the learners—can be modified on the fly by an experienced instructor. With e-learning, the learners and the instructional environment must be carefully examined to identify these issues at the outset and ensure that instruction is precisely tailored to learner and organizational needs. To use a construction metaphor, the analysis phase of ISD can be considered the foundation upon which the rest of instruction is built. Even the most flashy, expensive, and interactive course will fail without a solid analysis as its foundation.

Design

If the analysis phase is the foundation of ISD, the design phase is the architecture. Although most people recognize the importance of architectural design in the construction of a building, some expert pilots may feel that they could deliver an excellent course with minimal planning. Often, the belief that teaching is as simple as presenting information to learners results in instruction that consists of an unorganized collection of facts presented in a lecture. Teachers who fail to properly design their courses may believe that poor student progress is the fault of individual learners, rather than a reflection of the instructor's teaching style.

Thankfully, the science of ID offers significant insights into how adults learn, as well as ways of structuring content to facilitate learning. It is now known that lectures may work for rote memorization but not for critical thinking skills, which are particularly necessary for pilots. Chapter 9 includes suggestions on how to sequence content; choose between e-learning delivery methods (such as synchronous, asynchronous, or blended learning); effectively integrate media; and map out a course. This process creates a clear plan for instruction—similar to an architectural blueprint—and offers specific guidance on how effective instruction must be built.

Develop

To continue the construction metaphor, the development phase of ID is similar to the building of a structure: the required tradesmen and materials are gathered and the work begins. In the development phase of ID, the team required to build e-learning is assembled—including specialists in programming, project management, and graphic design—or an external contractor is hired. A choice is made about the interface and authoring tool, and the training course is built. Unlike the previous two phases of ISD, which incorporate a lot of educational theory, the develop phase is very practical in nature. The culmination of this phase is a course that is ready to deliver to learners.

Implement

The goal of the implement phase is to deliver the e-learning to pilots. However, several things should be considered before delivery. These include establishing the necessary information technology (IT) infrastructure, building an e-learning support structure (either electronically or by training employees to fulfil the role), and establishing an internal marketing campaign. The purpose of the internal marketing campaign is to manage the change from F2F to e-learning. Often, change is associated with anxiety. Instructors may worry that e-learning will replace them, or pilots may think that poor computer skills will cause them to fail a course. However, a company can manage the change through a process of educating employees and by giving them a chance to engage with training before it is fully integrated. Once such preliminaries have been completed, the training is ready to be integrated into daily operations, and the implementation of the e-learning can begin.

Evaluation

The final stage in the ADDIE model is evaluation. There are two types of evaluation: formative and summative. Formative evaluations take place while e-learning is being created, and are used by instructional designers to 'form' the course. Summative evaluations take place after e-learning has been delivered to learners, and are used by training managers, instructional designers, and company decision-makers to assess the effectiveness and impact of training. Although this stage is at the end of the ADDIE model, it is important to remember that the iterative nature of the model means that ID is never truly complete. The evaluation will identify areas of weakness, which will in turn lead to new analysis, design, development, and implementation, and eventually another evaluation.

Conclusion

The ADDIE ID model offers step-by-step guidance on how to create effective e-learning. Once an organization has decided that an e-learning course will be developed, it is tempting to immediately begin converting the slides and lecture notes from existing F2F courses into e-learning. This is a mistake. Imagine if a builder was given the materials and tools to build a structure and was asked to build it quickly without a proper foundation or any architectural blueprints. The end-product would probably be of very low quality. Similarly, it is crucial to complete a thorough ID process when developing e-learning. An organization that does not complete the important planning, organizational, implementation, and evaluation stages is taking a risk that their e-learning program will be completely ineffective.

Practical Summary

- The instructional design (ID) process can be used to produce training that specifically targets what people need to know and incorporates activities that help people learn.
- ID, also called instructional system design (ISD), is a systematic process of analyzing the need for instruction, designing the content, developing the course, implementing training within an organization, and evaluating its effectiveness:
    - This process forms the structure of the ADDIE model: analyze, design, develop, implement, evaluate.
    - ID begins with analysis, and works linearly through to evaluation. However, at the evaluation stage the process is iterative, meaning it repeats, cycling through another ADDIE process.

Chapter 8

Analysis

Measure twice,
cut once.

—Proverb

Overview

The purpose of this chapter is to review the components of the analysis phase of the instructional design (ID) process. This chapter will present the description and background theory of each component, accompanied by a practical step-by-step description or example of the process. Understanding how and when to use each element is perhaps best illustrated by considering the question that it answers:

- Is instruction necessary?
    - *Needs assessment* is a formal process of investigating whether training is needed, by exploring normative needs, felt needs, expressed needs, comparative needs, future needs, and critical incident needs.
    - This process is appropriate only for training that is optional, and not for training that is mandated by regulatory or pilot licensing requirements. ID for required training should begin at the performance assessment stage.
- What is the gap between current and ideal levels of performance?
    - *Performance assessment* is the formal process of investigating the gap between current and ideal performance. Its purpose is to ensure that training targets the problem, rather than its symptoms:
        o this process also investigates the source of the performance gap, as training is the solution only if people lack the skill or knowledge to do their job. Before training design begins, other possible sources of error must be considered, including problems with directions, feedback, tools and equipment, resources, and incentives and motivation.
- Once learners meet the ideal level of job performance, what indirect behaviors or attitudes may influence professional success?
    - *Goal assessment* is a process for identifying characteristics of a professional environment that are important, yet not directly linked to one's ability to carry out a task (such as professionalism, or a safety culture).

- Who are the learners? How might individual characteristics impact learning outcomes?
  - A *learner analysis* ensures that instruction is tailored toward the characteristics of the learners, resulting in training that is learner-centric.

  Where is the instruction to be delivered? Could environmental characteristics impact learning outcomes?
  - A *contextual analysis* examines the environment within which learning takes place, with the purpose of creating training that is relevant and appropriate in the professional context:
    - Important issues of instructional context include classroom seating, usability of equipment, organizational support, scheduling, transfer of training, and transfer context.
- Do you understand all of the tasks and subtasks required for ideal performance?
  - A *task analysis* is designed to break apart, analyze, and describe the knowledge, skills, and attitudes that training is meant to produce, making the characteristics of expert performance visible and understandable.
- Can you clearly articulate the knowledge, skills, and attitudes learners will have achieved once they have successfully completed training?
  - *Training objectives* clearly and unambiguously define the outcomes of training, but do not address how training is created (as this will be discussed in Chapter 9).

Introduction

The analysis portion of ID for e-learning is a crucial step that is too often overlooked or minimized. Although the analysis phase for e-learning does not significantly differ from the analysis phase for classroom-based instruction, the analysis phase for e-learning requires more time and attention. Unlike classroom instruction, which can be modified on the fly by a skilled instructor, e-learning instruction must be precisely tailored on the front end to fit the learning outcomes.

The analysis phase of instructional system design (ISD) is often contracted out to an e-learning development group, supported only by some course notes that are passed along by a training department. Unfortunately, asking an e-learning developer with no direct experience in aviation to perform this step is comparable to asking an actor who portrays a pilot on film to land an aircraft. The e-learning developer is skilled in delivering information and making it look attractive, but is not an expert in the subject area.

Therefore, instructional analysis is something that should always occur in-house before an e-learning developer is contracted. Working through this process will provide an aviation organization with clearly defined problems, learner characteristics, instructional analysis, objectives, and strategies. In-house analysis creates a solid foundation upon which effective e-learning can be developed, thus increasing the likelihood that the training will be effective.

Is Instruction Necessary?

Before beginning the ID process for a new computer-based course, it is important to first analyze what training an organization needs and—perhaps more importantly—when training is not needed. Training development consumes time, resources, and money. If it is possible to address the source of a recurring pilot error in another way, such as implementing a standard operating procedure (SOP) or mandatory crew rest, doing so is probably more advantageous than developing a new training program. Wickens et al. (2003) have suggested alternative interventions such as redesigning the physical environment (for example, lighting, temperature, or vibration of the cockpit); equipment (such as cockpit avionics or controls that may be difficult to operate); task (through new or revised SOPs); or selection (such as utilizing hiring practices to screen candidates and find those who are most likely to be successful on the job, which is common in military aviation). Depending on the situation and organization, alternative interventions may be more efficient. To avoid wasting company resources, it is important to investigate all possible interventions before beginning the ID process.

If it is determined that a secondary intervention, such as a new SOP, may ameliorate the recurrent error, supplementary training might be required. For example, if a new SOP is created, training may be required to familiarize pilots with the new procedure. Although this option does incorporate training, it will likely be less expensive than an attempt to solve the recurring error through an instructional intervention alone.

It is important to keep in mind that training does not refer exclusively to time spent in a classroom or in front of a computer. There are creative alternatives that allow training to be conducted on the job. For example, mobile learning technologies (m-learning) allow scenario-based training (SBT) to be e-mailed or sent via text messaging to pilots on their cellular phones or mobile devices. Thus pilots can consider a particular problem or scenario and respond at their convenience when time permits, refreshing the issue in their minds while reducing time at a training center. This strategy may lead to increased safety and productivity.

However, aviation is a unique industry, in which training is often regulated and therefore unavoidable. For mandatory training, it makes sense to fully invest the resources required to maximize the effectiveness and cost efficiency of instruction. It is important to consider training as an organizational investment, one that requires careful evaluation and planning.

Needs Assessment

When training is not mandatory by regulation, the organization should conduct a needs assessment to determine whether training is the most appropriate solution to a problem. Training will teach someone how to do something, but perhaps ignorance is not the reason why the person made a mistake. The mistake may be the result of negligence, fatigue, arrogance, or distractions. Training will not correct the mistake unless it specifically targets the cause of error. A needs assessment is a formal process of:

1. identifying discrepancies between what a person should be doing and what they actually are doing;
2. identifying the cause of the discrepancy;
3. prioritizing interventions that may solve the problem;
4. providing a baseline to measure the success of instruction (Bradshaw 1972).

There are six types of needs: normative, felt, expressed, comparative, anticipated, and critical incident (Burton and Merrill 1991; Morrison et al. 2004):

1. *Normative need.* A normative need exists when a person or group's level of performance is lower than an established standard. For example, a normative need would exist if a pilot demonstrated a level of performance below the standard for his or her license or rating.
2. *Felt need.* A felt need is an individual's desire to seek improvement. Felt needs can be identified by asking people what they want or need; however, keep in mind that responses may be biased by what is socially acceptable. For example, a felt need in aviation may be a pilot's desire to progress from a first officer position to captain. This felt need to progress to a captain's position may be based on the *need* for a higher salary to support one's family or the *desire* for authority on the flight deck.
3. *Expressed need.* An expressed need is the result of a felt need being acted upon. A general aviation (GA) pilot who experiences a felt need for increased flight safety may attend a single-pilot resource management (SRM) workshop in an effort to improve his or her skills. The act of the pilot attending the workshop is the expressed need.
4. *Comparative need.* A comparative need is the result of a group not having the same equipment or status as an external group. For example, an airline training department may express a *need* for a high-fidelity motion-based flight simulator because that is the type of training device most other airlines are using. It is important for instructional designers to determine what the comparative need is based on—the current training apparatus resulting in poorer performance compared with the industry standard, or simply a wish to keep up appearances.

5. *Future needs.* Unlike the needs already discussed, which focus on current training requirements, future needs refer to training shortcomings that are expected in the future. For example, if an airline expects delivery of a new type of aircraft in the future, it may begin to develop training programs before the aircraft joins the fleet. Assessing future needs is critical to ensure that an e-learning program is not obsolete by the time it is completed. Understanding this need allows organizations to prepare pilots for the environment as it will be, rather than how it is (Burton and Merrill 1991).
6. *Critical incident need.* The last type of need refers to critical incidents, meaning rare but devastating failures or emergencies with severe consequences. There are several critical incident needs in aviation. These include emergency procedures associated with system failures, security breaches, or physiological incapacitation.

Needs Assessment Process

Once a problem has been identified, it is important to determine whether there is a need for training to solve the problem, or if another solution may be a more efficient option. The following is a formal process that can be used to identify the needs of an organization. However, it is not always necessary to complete the process in its entirety. In general, one would only complete the entire process when trying to identify whether training should be used to address a problem or concern within a company. Since most aviation training is mandatory, an instructional designer would consider the various types of needs and discuss them with senior management and instructional staff to identify course improvements. An exception to this shortcut would occur if an entirely new course is being designed to address a specific problem—which was the case when crew resource management (CRM) was being introduced in the early 1980s. In such cases, it is important to conduct the formal needs assessment. The process is outlined below.

Phase 1: Planning

1. Identify target group. The first step in conducting a needs analysis is to determine specifically what job position or group of people you are interested in.
2. Define questions that need to be answered. Considering the six types of need, identify key questions that need to be answered by the population. These questions will relate to the type of training that is being designed.
3. Data network. Next, assess who is available to answer questions or surveys. Keep in mind that in addition to the target group, you may solicit feedback from management, instructors, line operation staff, and so on. You may also seek data from nonhuman sources such as safety databases or performance records. Specific types of needs are best addressed by certain

groups. For example, pilots should be asked directly about their felt needs. Performance records are a good source for assessing normative needs. Lastly, management is in the best position to describe future needs.
4. Data collection tools. Finally, you need to design surveys, questionnaires, and interview scripts, and to define how databases and records will be assessed.

Phase 2: Data Collection

In this phase, the data collection tools will be distributed throughout your network, interviews will be conducted, and databases will be reviewed. It is not feasible to interview or survey everyone who could be impacted by training. Rather, focus on a representative portion of the group. For example, if the training will be delivered to pilots at several hub airports, make sure that a few from each hub are included in the data collection process.

Phase 3: Analysis and Reporting

1. Analyze and prioritize needs. Once all of the pertinent data have been collected, they must be reviewed and prioritized. Depending on the organization, the prioritization of needs may be based on different issues, such as a ranking scale, cost to the organization, impact (number of people affected), how frequently a specific need was identified, or a timeline (Morrison et al. 2004)
2. Report production. The final step of the needs analysis is the documentation of how the process was conducted, what the analysis identified, and the final recommendations. This report may identify that training is an appropriate intervention, or that another approach may be more advantageous (for example, equipment redesign or revised selection procedures).

Performance Assessment

Whereas a needs assessment focuses on the organization and employee groups, a performance assessment investigates the gap between an individual's actual performance and how the individual should be performing. The purpose of a performance assessment is to ensure that a training intervention focuses specifically on the underlying problem, rather than on its symptoms (Morrison et al. 2004).

The following scenario illustrates the importance of a performance assessment in determining whether training will solve a problem. The chief pilot of a small flight school notices that students returning from long cross-country flights continually make errors during their final landings. Clearly, there is a performance gap between an error-free landing and what the students are demonstrating. The chief pilot's initial response is to tell the flight instructors to spend more time teaching the students landing skills. However, a performance assessment reveals another cause for these errors. The school's policy is to schedule student cross-country flights at 6 a.m., to avoid the poor weather that typically rolls into the area around noon. The assessment reveals that the students are not used to waking up so early, so they are tired when they begin their flights and completely fatigued after their final landing. Accordingly, the school changes its cross-country scheduling policy and distributes information to the students on proper sleep habits and fatigue management.

Training is the solution to the problem only if people do not have the skills or knowledge they need to do the job correctly. In the above situation, the students possessed the knowledge and skills required for landing. Therefore, any additional training time spent reviewing landing skills would have wasted time and money and would not have solved the problem. Before you design a training program, consider these other possible sources of error (adapted from Piskurich 2006):

1. *Directions*. Mistakes may be made because people are ignorant of the most effective way to do the job or are unable to find the reference material they need:
   - Are aircraft checklists easy to find, up-to-date, and understandable?
2. *Feedback*. Another source of problems is improper feedback from superiors:
   - Are you comfortable asking your chief pilot questions?
   - Are your questions answered constructively and in a timely manner?
3. *Tools and equipment*. Aviators rely heavily on the equipment they use. If something as simple as a pilot's pen fails to work, the distraction and frustration can lead to mistakes. If a particular system is difficult to use, confusing, or glitchy, it should be identified and replaced.
   - Are you comfortable using all of the onboard systems?
   - Is there any equipment that you think is poorly designed?
4. *Resources*. Pilots need access to a significant amount of resources, both for preflight planning and on the flight deck.
   - Do you have any problems communicating with air traffic control?
   - Do you have all of the materials you need to do your job?
   - Are there any factors in your work environment that make your job more difficult?
5. *Incentives and motivation*. Another source of error may be that pilots are not rewarded for putting in extra effort, or their level of motivation is low.
   - Are you satisfied with your current salary, compared with the industry standard?
   - Are there performance-based incentives or bonuses?
   - Can you think of any negative consequences associated with poor performance?
   - Do you have an internal desire to do your job properly (Piskurich 2006)?

If an assessment reveals that error is associated with lack of directions, feedback, tools, resources, incentives, or motivation, it probably cannot be fixed by a training program. However, problems are typically associated with more than one issue. A combination of remedies, such as training and financial incentives, may be the best solution.

Goal Assessment

Once a performance assessment has been completed, it will be clear how a specific group's performance compares to an ideal level of performance. For example, as a trainer you may identify that a group of instructors have poor inter-rater reliability (IRR). IRR refers to the consistency between instructor scores for students who demonstrate the same performance level; ideally, scores should be consistent across instructors within an organization. You develop an instructor training course that will standardize grading, ensuring that all instructors utilize the same grading criteria and assign grades equivalent to the industry standard. Eventually the training is completed and the company's instructors are demonstrating excellent IRR. Then you are approached by the general manager, who comments that the training program does not promote the professionalism, safety culture, or motivation that is required—even though the instructor performance now meets the desired standard! Obviously, this can be a very frustrating situation for a training designer. However, the general manager is not incorrect. There are often characteristics of a professional environment that are very important, yet not directly linked to one's ability to carry out a task. For example, an instructor who grades students precisely to the criteria described in training has accomplished the goals of the IRR program. However, he or she may have a very negative attitude that discourages students, lack professionalism in their dress and deportment, be completely void of leadership and problem-solving abilities, and continually cut corners with regard to safety. The purpose of a goal assessment is to consider all of these tangential, yet important, personal characteristics.

There are two situations in which a goal assessment will be conducted:

1. After a needs assessment, to identify the instructional priorities.
2. In lieu of a needs assessment:
    - Quite often, a training designer will be told of a need and asked to design training to target the need. In this situation, a needs analysis is not required because the need has already been identified. Instead, a goal analysis can be conducted to determine how training can target the key characteristics that require improvement (Morrison et al. 2004).

The purpose of the goal analysis is to specify which observable characteristics of human performance demonstrate that a goal has been accomplished. A training designer can turn to a goal analysis at any point where he or she identifies a problem for which there is no clear fix. For example, how can I motivate the learners, how can I explain a concept so that they will understand, how can I make them appreciate a safety culture (Mager 1997)?

Goal Analysis Process (adapted from Morrison et al. 2004)

1. Identify an aim:
    - Using feedback from the organization, determine what problems need to be addressed. Once the problem has been identified, describe an aim. The aim should describe a performance characteristic associated with the goal. If the problem is that flight instructors must demonstrate a safety culture, one aim would be the ability to conduct an effective safety culture briefing for students.
2. Set goals:
    - If the goal is achieved, what specific activities will be occurring? Specific goals must be created, based on the aim identified in the previous section. The best strategy for this section is to brainstorm as many goals as possible. Don't worry about duplications or tangents, as these will be sorted out later. The following is an example of a rough list generated through brainstorming.
    To conduct an effective safety culture, briefing instructors must:
    – outline the briefing;
    – describe a good safety culture;
    – describe a bad safety culture;
    – describe the importance of a safety culture;
    – describe the impact of an effective safety culture on a company's financial success;
    – organize safety reports;
    – maintain a database of safety records;
    – describe how an effective safety culture improves a company's safety record;
    – describe the regulatory justification for a safety culture;
    – describe the key attributes which are observable within an effective safety culture;
    – know the importance of voluntary incident reporting;
    – show the willingness of students and instructors to submit voluntary incident reports.
3. Refine goals:
    - Once the rough list has been created, clarify the goals by eliminating those that are repetitions or not feasible, by combining goals, and by clarifying goals that are unclear:
    – effectively organize briefing material;
    – identify characteristics of an effective and ineffective safety culture;

    – explain why a safety culture is important to a company, on the basis of regulations and statistics demonstrating financial and safety impacts;
    – organize and maintain safety report database;
    – promote key attributes that are observable within an effective safety culture, such as voluntary incident reporting.
4. Rank goals:
   - Organize the list of goals according to whatever criterion is most appropriate to the training situations (such as importance, risk, or cost). Some goals may be eliminated, if they are not feasible with regard to resources available to accomplish the goal, or the knowledge required:
     i. identify characteristics of an effective and an ineffective safety culture;
     ii. explain why a safety culture is important to a company, on the basis of regulations and statistics demonstrating financial and safety impacts;
     iii. promote key attributes that are observable within an effective safety culture, such as voluntary incident reporting;
     iv. organize and maintain safety report database;
     v. effectively organize briefing material.
5. Refine goals again:
   - Review the list of goals, while referencing the characteristics of the job and specific purpose of training:
     – Goal iv was deleted because the safety reporting database is not accessible to students.
6. Make a final ranking:
   - Review and prepare the final ranking of goals, considering how important each goal is to the learner's ability to perform the task. This final ranking will be used to design training:
     i. Identify characteristics of an effective and ineffective safety culture.
     ii. Explain why a safety culture is important to a company, on the basis of regulations and statistics demonstrating financial and safety impacts.
     iii. Promote key attributes that are observable within an effective safety culture, such as voluntary incident reporting.
     iv. Effectively organize briefing material.

Learner Analysis

From an ID perspective, it is crucial that training be geared toward the characteristics of the learners. For example, a new flight instructor may prepare a detailed ground school lesson on instrument procedures. Inevitably, the flight instructor's training course will be based on the knowledge he or she thinks students need to know. However, if the learners have no aviation experience, the material will be too advanced for them and they will become cognitively overloaded (and likely very frustrated). The opposite is also true. If the unfortunate instructor's classroom is filled with airline transport pilots with skills far beyond the lesson, the pilots may find the lesson extremely boring and difficult to pay attention to. Clearly, training is not just about the content but also about the people who are meant to learn it. The process of tailoring the training to the skills of the learners results in *learner-centric* training. This is different from traditional instruction, which can be considered *instructor-centric*. The majority of aviation training becomes *instructor-centric* because as instructors develop their own expertise, they begin to assume that everyone learns the same way they do. So, instructors explain new concepts in the way they understand them, with familiar examples and a delivery method that they are comfortable with. This results in instruction that may not be well understood by the learners. The instructors' familiarity with the material may also cause them to over- or underexplain concepts (Smith and Ragan 2005). A learner analysis, as a component of a systematic ID model, ensures that the instruction is not based upon one person's guess of what the students need to know.

With computer-based training (CBT), performing a learner analysis is particularly important. A classroom instructor may intuitively adapt the difficulty or content of material as a result of interaction and observation of learners. In e-learning, however, it is necessary to consider these factors on the front end and to design courses that are either (1) well-suited to a specific group of learners; or (2) adaptive, so that complexity adjusts according to learner performance. The learner analysis must also consider the students' comfort with computers and their familiarity with computers. In addition, for CBT to be accepted by learners, it must also be visually appealing. For example, when training is geared toward professional aviators, it is crucial that animations do not look too cute or juvenile, as this may offend learners and distract them from the goals of the learning program.

However, some may wonder whether it is worthwhile to invest time and resources into a learner analysis. After all, the learner demographics in aviation are less diverse than those in other industries. The base requirements of pilot licensing and minimum job selection criteria filter the group of learners, ensuring a minimum level of flight experience. In addition, whereas in other disciplines meeting the needs of learners with disabilities is a major challenge in e-learning, in aviation the pilot medical requirements ensure that there are no learners with disabilities.

Although pilots share many characteristics, it is important to look more deeply into key learner characteristics, including:

- interests;
- male–female ratio;
- age;
- level of motivation toward the course material;

- feelings toward the work environment (including job stability);
- geographic location;
- culture;
- level of education;
- time pressure to complete training;
- family life and other external responsibilities;
- attitudes;
- predispositions.

However, the most important learner characteristic to assess is what learners already know about the material you plan to include in the training. Remember, whatever amount of time you spend thinking about the content of a course, spending even a fraction of that time assessing the learners can dramatically improve the quality of instruction.

Another learner characteristic that may be influential is culture. Each individual is influenced by three distinct cultures while on the job: professional, organizational, and national. These cultures can positively or negatively impact the effectiveness of training, and each is an important consideration in the design process. The *professional culture* refers to the norms and values of aviation, which are passed down from senior pilots to new recruits. Aviation is characterized by a strong professional culture, which directly relates to enjoyment of one's work. For example, when 12,500 pilots from 19 countries were asked to respond to the question 'I like my job' on a 5-point Likert scale (with 5 indicating *agree strongly* and 1 indicating *disagree strongly*), the average score was 4.7, meaning that 92 percent of respondents either agree or agree strongly with the statement (Helmreich and Merritt 1998). Therefore, it is reasonable to assume that pilots like their job in aviation. The ID can capitalize on this intrinsic motivation toward aviation.

However, the fact that pilots like their job does not necessarily mean that they like the organization they work for. In fact, organizational culture is quite separate from professional culture. An *organizational culture* can be defined as 'the values, beliefs, assumptions, rituals, symbols and behaviors that define a group' (Helmreich and Merritt 1998: 109). Some of these characteristics, such as symbols, are directly visible and include company uniforms and logos. Other aspects of organizational culture are not direclty observable; these include values, which define what is important and what is not. Although pilots like their job, the percentage who said they were proud to work for their company ranged from 26 percent at one U.S. regional airline to 97 percent at a major United States carrier (Helmreich and Merritt 1998). Therefore, levels of extrinsic motivation might vary between organizations. It is important to consider such factors when designing instruction, so that the design and values of the training will be appropriate to the organizational culture.

The final cultural aspect to consider is potentially the most difficult to address in the ID process. Although the professional culture of aviation exerts a very powerful influence on pilot attitude and behavior, each pilot is also influenced by his or her national culture (Helmreich and Merritt 1998). *National culture* refers to the values of groups of individuals who come from a particular country. When early CRM training was developed in the United States and shipped overseas, the results surprised researchers. The varying performance of pilots from different countries on CRM courses revealed that piloting an aircraft was about more than technical hands-on skills. Rather, it became clear that national culture may impact cockpit performance (Helmreich and Merritt 1998). Some of the cultural variations include:

- Conflict resolution:
    - methods of conflict resolution range from confrontation to compromises to complete avoidance.
- Definition of effective leadership skills:
    - the same leadership behavior may be considered harsh or encouraging, depending on the culture.
- Communication styles:
    - the term *Yes* might mean 'affirmative' in one culture and simply 'I hear you' in another culture.
- Social interactions:
    - confusion can arise from various cultural influences and behaviors, including misreading of emotions, improper apologies, or inappropriate familiarity—such as calling a crewmate by his first name (Helmreich and Merritt 1998).

From the e-learning perspective, other cultural considerations include the prevalence of computer technology, mobile devices, and CBT within the national culture. Although a complete review of aviation national culture is beyond the scope of this text, readers are referred to Helmreich and Merritt (1998) for an excellent review of national culture in relation to aviation.

For design purposes, once the key learner characteristics have been identified, the question of how to gather information about learner characteristics remains. Options include surveying a sample of students and questioning current teachers. As a last resort, instruction can be based on the job requirements or selection process (for example, by assuming that learners already know certain things because they have an airline transport pilot license). The last option is the most risky. For example, experience in aviation is based on the pilot's total number of flying hours. Yet, two pilots with 5,000 hours will likely have been exposed to vastly different situations, environments, and aircraft. Therefore it is risky to base instruction upon the assumption that 'the average pilot with 5,000 hours will know . . .'. The ultimate question is whether a pilot has 5,000 unique hours of experience, with exposure to many novel situations and challenges, or just the same hour of experience repeated 5,000 times. In addition, pilots with equal levels of experience may have forgotten previously learned information, or they might have had little exposure to certain flight characteristics (such as actual instrument meteorological conditions (IMC)), or their skills may have degraded. ID must consider that significant variations will exist among a group of learners with the same level of experience.

The results of a learner analysis will impact several instructional decisions, including:

- at what level of difficulty to begin training;
- how to motivate learners and convince them of the importance of instruction;
- choosing appropriate content;
- development and sequence of objectives;
- degree of detail and the level of the material;
- appropriate media;
- level of learner control, including ability to repeat or skip ahead within lessons;
- vocabulary and reading level;
- amount of instruction that can be chunked together without overwhelming learners;
- type and amount of guidance and help prompts that must be included in lesson;
- choice of practice activities;
- type and amount of feedback (Morrison et al. 2004; Smith and Ragan 2005).

Learner Analysis: The Process

Phase 1: Planning

- Identify which learner characteristics may impact learning, and prepare surveys, questionnaires, or interview scripts:
    – examples of key characteristics include questions about interests, gender, age, geographic location, level of education, cultural background, family life and other external responsibilities, level of motivation toward the course material, feelings about the work environment, and, most importantly, what learners already know about the material you plan to train.

Phase 2: Data Collection

- Distribute data collection instruments (surveys, questionnaires):
    – to ensure that survey responses are reliable, allow them to be submitted anonymously, or guarantee confidentiality.

- Conduct interviews when necessary:
  - if unable to access current students, interview instructors about learner characteristics.

Phase 3: Analysis and Reporting

- Once the data has been collected, conduct an analysis:
  - a helpful method of organizing numerical data is to plot the characteristics on a range from high to low, along with the mean. Example: Learners range in age from 18 to 59, with a mean age of 33.
  - non-numerical data should be analyzed and written into a brief statement. Example: The majority of learners (82 percent) are from a Western background including Canada and the United States. In decreasing order, the other students come from Chinese, Indian, and Brazilian descent.
- When the analysis has been completed, a final report should be written detailing key learner characteristics that will impact training effectiveness, including justification for why the chosen characteristics are important.

Contextual Analysis

> Context is everything.
>
> —Jonassen 1993

Once learner characteristics have been identified, it is important to analyze the context within which learning will take place. This analysis is based upon contextual learning theory, which suggests that learning can only take place when new knowledge makes sense to learners and relates to their past experiences (Hull 1993). Therefore, e-learning should be designed in such a way that learners interact with scenarios and problems that resemble real-world situations. Contextual learning theory is the foundation of problem-based learning (PBL). Rather than giving learners lists of information to memorize, PBL presents a real-world situation and requires the learners to think it through and devise a solution. PBL may increase retention of knowledge, enhance transfer of concepts to new problems, increase interest in the subject being taught, and improve self-directed learning skills (Norman and Schmidt 1992). Overall, learning is inextricably influenced by the context within which it is taught. That context can either promote or inhibit learning.

Therefore, effective e-learning should try to replicate the real-world environment within which the new knowledge will be used. However, before this can take place, a contextual analysis should be performed.

Tessmer and Richey (1997) define *context* as 'a multilevel body of factors in which learning and performance are embedded' (87). Three levels of context are orienting, instructional, and transfer context. The *orienting context* refers to learner characteristics (which were discussed previously in the chapter), specifically intellectual capabilities, and motivation to learn. The *instructional context* is the environment directly involved in the training being delivered, including the physical and social environment. Lastly, *transfer context* is the environment within which the learning will be utilized.

Instructional Context Characteristics

Classroom seating   One of the most researched aspects of contextual learning is classroom seating. The majority of this research is not directly applicable to the design of e-learning. However, research does suggest that seating comfort impacts one's performance and ability to maintain attention (Bailey 1982; Gay 1986; Tessmer and Harris 1992). Therefore, before an e-learning program is deployed within an organization, it may be helpful to disseminate information regarding how to create an ideal workspace, including the importance of a comfortable chair.

Usability   Another contextual factor to consider is the usability of the equipment. From an e-learning perspective, the two main considerations are: (1) the usability of the computer, and (2) the usability of the software. If the computer the learner is using is out of date, the Internet connection is poor, the peripherals (such as mouse or touchpad) are unfamiliar, or the speaker volume is too low or high, the learner may focus more attention on the equipment than on the learning material itself. In addition, careful consideration must be paid to the electronic environment created within the training program, to ensure ease of use and a familiar, professional context. In the professional culture of the aviation industry, it would be inappropriate to use pink backgrounds or unusual italicized fonts. Keep in mind that you have control over creating the learning context within the e-learning program, so it is your responsibility to ensure that it is characteristic of the real-world environment.

Organizational support   Another contextual factor is the organizational support for the e-learning program. In order for any training program to be accepted and applied by learners within an organization, it is crucial that the learners sense management's support for the training. Unfortunately, a 'lack of management support for CRM and a failure by such evaluators as line check airmen to reinforce its practice' is one reason why acceptance of this type of training tends to decrease over time, even with recurrent training (Helmreich, Merritt and Wilheim 1999: 24–5). Therefore, assessing managerial support for training is an important step in the contextual analysis. This assessment should include reviewing the organizational culture, the system of reward and punishment, and group attitudes toward e-learning. The assessment should also attempt to determine the type of personality that is sought by the organization. For example, over the past 30 years there has been a shift toward a cooperative approach to aviation. This shift is evidenced by CRM training and its emphasis on communication and collaboration among everyone involved in flight operations, from pilots to flight attendants, dispatchers, and mechanics. An e-learning instructional designer should understand this cultural context and try to create training that fosters cooperative strategies and interaction among employee groups.

Scheduling Scheduling can also be a challenge, as a 45-minute e-learning session may actually take a learner more than an hour when the time to prepare materials and log in to the training system are factored in. This is an important consideration when training is a job requirement and learners are paid for training. If learners are compensated only for the time spent logged in to the training program, there may be hostility, particularly if gaining access to the training is a lengthy process.

Transfer Context

Transfer of training Transfer of training is defined as the application of knowledge and skills gained in training to the real-world environment (Machin 2002). However, not all transfer is positive. There are actually three types of training transfer: (1) positive transfer, (2) negative transfer, and (3) zero transfer. *Positive transfer* occurs when training helps the learner acquire a skill more quickly than learners who did not receive training—for example, when an aviation student who completes computer-based learning (CBL) on an aircraft procedure gains proficiency on that procedure with less time in the aircraft than students who did not complete training. *Negative transfer* occurs when training reduces a learner's ability to gain a new skill. For example, if e-learning is very poorly designed, a student may learn procedures incorrectly, or pick up a bad habit that requires additional aircraft training before becoming proficient in a new skill. Lastly, *zero transfer* refers to training that has no impact on the learner's ability to acquire new skills. Instructional designers work hard to avoid the latter two types of transfer. However, negative and zero transfer are more common than one might expect. Unfortunately, some suggest that as little as 10 percent of training transfers into the real-world workplace (Georgenson 1982). Ineffective training wastes the company's money and the learner's time.

In addition, researchers often distinguish between near-transfer and far-transfer tasks (Merriam and Leahy 2005). If the training environment is very similar to real-world situations, it is more likely that positive transfer will occur. This type of training, considered *near transfer*, focuses on the learner's ability to replicate specific skills. By comparison, *far-transfer* tasks teach the foundational principles along with specific skills (Royer 1979). The purpose of far-transfer training is to provide students with the ability to apply their knowledge to novel situations, beyond what the instructional designer has been able to predict.

Transfer context Instructional context—the environment in which the training is meant to be applied—can significantly impact transfer of training. Although the context is a less obvious contributor to transfer than learner characteristics or training content, it is equally important (McKeogh, Lupart and Marini 1996). Context impacts transfer because it may impact learner motivation, or because it may not provide opportunities to practice new skills (Tessmer and Richey 1997). To support transfer, instructional designers should try to:

- provide opportunities for the learner to practice applying new skills in a real-world context;
- motivate the learner to apply the new skills;
- ensure that the organization provides social support and incentives to support the training (Tessmer and Richey 1997).

Contextual Analysis Process (adapted from Tessmer and Richey 1997)

Phase 1: Planning

1. Establish the training parameters, including the need for training, desired outcomes, learner characteristics, resources, and limitations.
2. Identify the orienting, instructional, and transfer context factors that you think are relevant to the current training program.
3. Determine how data can be collected:
   - there are several options available for data collection, including surveys, interviews, and observations.
4. Create data collection tools and techniques.

Phase 2: Data Collection

1. Using data collection tools, gather information on orienting, learning, and transfer context factors.
2. Identify factors that may *inhibit* learning (unsupportive attitude of management, poor computer skills of learners, uncomfortable computer lab, and so on).
3. Identify factors that may be *missing* (lack of computer lab, no wireless Internet access available, no incentives, and so on).
4. Identify factors that may *support* learning (student motivation toward new technology, flexibility of web-based learning, and so on).
5. Outline the relationships between factors that inhibit, are missing from, or support learning within all three contexts (orienting, learning, and transfer).

Phase 3: Analysis and Reporting

1. Determine how success of instruction will be measured (for example, transfer, organizational impact).
2. Mitigate inhibiting factors (for example, distribute a computer skills course to those learners who need it).
3. Install missing factors (for example, install a wireless Internet connection in common work areas, design organizational incentives for training completion).
4. Exploit facilitative factors (for example, ensure that training meets expectations of motivated learners and that web-based training (WBT) is always accessible).
5. Monitor contextual factors during implementation of the course.

Task Analysis

Once the planning steps described earlier in this chapter have been completed, the instructional designer should complete a task analysis, which is probably the most important stage in the ID process. This process is the intellectual foundation of ID (Jonassen, Tessmer and Hannum 1999). Unfortunately, it is also the least understood component of the ISD process. A task analysis allows the training designer to break apart, understand, and describe the learning that the training is meant to produce. Fundamentally, if you cannot articulate or understand how learners should act and think following instruction, how can you expect the training to have the desired effect?

The purpose of a task analysis is to make the characteristics of expert performance visible and understandable. The characteristics of expert performance are made visible by describing the:

- goals of learning;
- real-world components of the job (including how people act and what they are thinking);
- type of knowledge used on the job (such as declarative, structural, or procedural);
- skills, tasks, or goals that should be taught;
- tasks that are of the highest priority;
- sequence in which tasks are performed and, therefore, should be learned;
- design of instructional activities and techniques that promote learning;
- selection of appropriate media and learning structure (such as synchronous vs. asynchronous e-learning);
- design of assessment and evaluation tools (Jonassen, Tessmer and Hannum 1999).

Too often, instruction is designed by someone who possesses operational experience but no direct knowledge of how to conduct a task analysis. Instructors may hope that the resulting training will produce the desired learning outcomes, but it is ultimately a shot in the dark. Problems can also arise from management who desire effective training but are not willing to commit the staff time required to complete an appropriate task analysis.

Unfortunately, one perfect approach does not exist. Rather, each solution is associated with beliefs regarding learning and instruction. There are five types of analysis: procedural, learning, cognitive, activity, and subject matter. The training designer must decide which type(s) of analysis to perform. Unfortunately, most courses use a single task analysis method. Approximately two-thirds of task analyses conducted in the real world use a procedural approach, because this is the only task analysis approach that many instructional designers know. The usual result is procedurally oriented instruction that may not fit the needs of the learner (Jonassen, Tessmer and Hannum 1999).

The Five Task Analysis Approaches

1. *Procedural.* A procedural analysis focuses on breaking down basic components of a job, and describing each component.
2. *Learning.* Learning analysis takes a more psychological approach, investigating how learners process information while conducting a task.
3. *Cognitive.* The cognitive task analysis (CTA) approach emerged from learning analyses. CTA has become increasingly popular in recent years, fueled by military training and by research into human–computer interaction. CTA uses a specific set of techniques to describe which mental strategies and knowledge are used to successfully complete a task.
4. *Activity.* Human activity task analyses apply anthropological methods to learning. This approach is related to contextual learning (described earlier in this chapter, in the discussion on contextual analysis). The activity task analysis investigates how people do their jobs in their real-world settings, with consideration given to the social and cultural environment of the workplace.
5. *Subject matter.* A subject matter approach to task analysis focuses on the structure and organization of the material to be taught. This is accomplished by examining the elements of the learning material and identifying relationships among these concepts (Jonassen, Tessmer and Hannum 1999).

So, how does one choose which task analysis approach is most appropriate for any given situation? It is nearly impossible for professional instructional designers to develop expertise in all types of task analysis. Therefore, it is unrealistic to expect that aviation trainers, who are not dedicated to ID full time, will possess the expertise to make this decision. Therefore, a decision matrix, adapted from

Jonassen, Tessmer and Hannum (1999), has been developed to help a trainer work through the decision. The decision matrix is presented in Table 8.1.

Table 8.1   Task analysis decision matrix

		Procedural	Learning	Cognitive	Activity	Subject Matter
Type of instruction being designed						
	Procedural	X				
	Direct instruction		X			
	Problem solving or guided learning			X		
	Constructivist				X	
	Content, subject, or topic-oriented					X
Within what context will the instruction be delivered?						
	Workplace	X				
	Direct instruction		X			X
	Constructivist learning environments			X	X	
	Information retrieval					X

Source: Adapted from Jonassen, Tessmer and Hannum 1999.

Although the process varies among the five types of task analyses, all five types include five distinct functions: task inventory, selection, description, sequencing, and classifying learning outcomes (adapted from Jonassen, Tessmer and Hannum 1999):

1. *Task inventory.* This is a listing of tasks that are relevant to ID (Jonassen, Tessmer and Hannum 1999).

2. *Task selection.* This function involves choosing, from the task inventory, the tasks for which training should be developed. Available priorities should be assigned to tasks on the basis of constraints such as resources, current level of learners, and the likelihood that training will solve the problem. The result of this phase is the final list of training objectives (Jonassen, Tessmer and Hannum 1999).
3. *Task description.* This process involves a more detailed breakdown of the tasks in the inventory. These are deconstructed, as thoroughly as possible, into tasks, knowledge required for the tasks, and objectives of the tasks (Jonassen, Tessmer and Hannum 1999).
4. *Task sequencing.* This phase involves the sequencing of the task, not just in the way it is performed in a real-world environment, but in how the instruction is sequenced. Very often, the sequence of the task in the real world is the most logical approach to training. However, this is not always the case. The sequence may be based on teaching underlying skills before those of a higher level. The elaboration theory argues for a general-to-specific sequence, while situated learning is based on learning simultaneous and underlying tasks. The sequence chosen depends on the instructional assumptions made (Jonassen, Tessmer and Hannum 1999).
5. *Classifying learning outcomes.* The last phase involves classifying the important knowledge and skills learners require into specific learning outcomes. What knowledge, skills, and attitudes do learners require to accomplish the task? The outcomes of this phase ensure compatibility between tasks and their assessments (such as tests or assignments) and between tasks and method of instruction. This phase also helps with sequencing, ensuring that simple prerequisite skills are taught before advanced tasks (Jonassen, Tessmer and Hannum 1999)

Although there are applications for each kind of task analysis in aviation, a detailed review of all five processes is beyond the scope of this text. The reader is referred to Jonassen, Tessmer and Hannum (1999) for a detailed description of all five types of task analysis. However, for the purpose of illustration, the steps involved in a procedural task analysis are outlined below. Keep in mind that the procedural task analysis, although by far the most popular type of task analysis, is best used for analyzing procedural tasks (for example, SOPs). This approach is not suitable for analyzing cognitive or social tasks, such as those associated with CRM training.

Procedural Task Analysis

A procedure is a sequence of tasks that learners must master in order to complete a task successfully. In aviation, SOPs are commonly used to standardize the way pilots within a company perform a specific maneuver. The easiest way to understand a task analysis is to consider how a SOP is written. Typically, expert pilots would carefully think through all of the tasks and subtasks that a pilot must complete to execute a maneuver in the most effective manner. Voila! These expert pilots have completed a procedural task analysis, probably without knowing the official process for doing so. Therefore, this process should not be perceived as overwhelming, as any aviation professional is capable of conducting a procedural task analysis. This section will present some strategies and guidance material to maximize the efficiency of analyses. Keep in mind that a procedural analysis focuses only on observable tasks—tasks that can be visually observed. Other tasks associated with attitudes or thought processes (such as decision making or problem solving) are considered in other task analysis approaches (see Jonassen, Tessmer and Hannum 1999 for a broad overview, or Seamster, Redding and Kaempf 1997 for a review of CTA in aviation). Again, before one begins a task analysis it is crucial to consider what type of learning is required. A procedural approach is most appropriate for the instruction of procedures!

The best way to conduct a procedural analysis is through a task observation while the work is being performed in the actual work environment. Because of financial or environmental constraints, however, observing the task in real time may not always be a feasible option. For example, when designing SOPs for emergency procedures, it is not logical for the pilot and training designer to create a real emergency situation in-flight, because of the risk involved. For this reason, flight simulators can be ideal for conducting a task analysis. Keep in mind, however, that the thought processes of a pilot in a simulator may be significantly different from those in an actual emergency condition, in which fear, anxiety, or unanticipated malfunctions may occur.

Before beginning the task observation, the instructional designer must create a task inventory and perform a task selection. The task inventory will list all of the tasks a person must perform to accomplish a procedure successfully. The task selection will narrow the list to those tasks that are likely to be improved through training. The next step is a task description, which is conducted while observing the task in real time. During the task observation, the instructional designer's job is to document precise task descriptions detailing all of the tasks and subtasks that must be performed to complete the procedure successfully. The instructional designer will typically start with the broad general tasks and then break them apart to identify the subtasks. There are three questions that can be used to guide the task description process (Morrison et al. 2004):

1. What actions must the person take to accomplish the task?
    - dialing in frequencies, moving flight controls, pressing buttons or flipping switches, verbally confirming actions with another flight crewmember, and so on.
2. What knowledge must the person have, before beginning the task, in order to complete it successfully?
    - knowledge of systems and components, general airmanship, ability to use the radio, and so on.

3. What environmental cues are available to inform the person that the task has been completed successfully, that there is a problem, or that a different task should be completed?
   - warning and caution messages on flight deck, external environment (including ramp personnel and equipment, or weather and traffic at altitude), location of toggle switches, radio and transponder displays, and so on.

Task descriptions are often presented in flowcharts, visually describing the flow of a decision-making process. In aviation, task descriptions more commonly take the form of step-by-step checklists. For example, a task description for an airline pilot completing a pre-takeoff procedure may indicate that to successfully complete the procedure, the pilot must complete the following tasks:

- check that the brake temperature is in the green range;
- set the bleeds, packs, and cross-bleeds to takeoff configuration;
- notify the flight attendants that the cabin must be ready for takeoff;
- ensure that no warning or caution messages are presented on the engine indicating and crew alerting system (EICAS);
- acknowledge any advisory messages on the EICAS;
- check that the appropriate power mode is indicated on the EICAS;
- ensure that the transponder is set on the assigned code by checking the display;
- select the traffic advisory (TA)/resolution advisory (RA) position on the transponder;
- set the traffic collision avoidance system (TCAS) to the appropriate range;
- set the aircraft to takeoff configuration;
- crosscheck the onboard fuel quantity against the required release fuel for the trip;
- turn on the landing and strobe lights.

Keep in mind that all of these tasks contain verbs, or 'action words,' such as *check*, *notify*, and *turn on*. If any tasks that have been identified do not contain verbs, consider revising their wording—or reconsider them altogether, as they might not be tasks at all. Observation is an excellent method of collecting data for a task description. However, it is also important to speak with or survey other trainers and line-workers to gather additional information about aspects of the job that might not be visible. The following are some of the questions you might ask these individuals:

- What aspect of your job is most enjoyable?
- What shortcuts or rules of thumb do you use on the job that improves your efficiency?
- What aspects of job performance do you think new hires are the worst at?

- What training or experience has best prepared you to succeed in your job?
- What challenges or problems do you encounter most often (Piskurich 2006)?

Once tasks have been identified, it is time to explore other aspects of the task description. These include time available to complete the task; contingency items (what to do in the event one of the tasks becomes impractical); environmental cues such as fog (strobe lights should not be used in low visibility conditions, as they may cause distraction); a detailed description of how the task is physically carried out (pilot will use right hand to select transponder mode); and feedback from instrument displays or from first officer responses (Jonassen, Tessmer and Hannum 1999).

Once a task description is complete, the next step is task sequencing. The purpose of this phase is to identify the cognitive requirements for each task, that is, the knowledge and skills that the user must possess before the task can be attempted. For example, the task may require a learner to possess a massive amount of background knowledge that novice learners cannot be expected to have. Once the cognitive requirements for each task have been determined, the tasks will be organized and sequenced for training development.

The final phase of the procedural task analysis process is the classification of learning outcomes. This phase is based on the list of tasks created in the previous steps, and involves classifying the specific knowledge, skills, and attitudes required to accomplish the tasks. This is a crucial process, as it defines specifically what learners should know and what attitudes and hands-on skills they should have once they have completed training. The findings from this phase will also be used to develop evaluation tools (such as tests to measure learning). This task analysis phase is very similar to the final step in the analysis section of ID for e-learning: the writing of training objectives. In fact, the work done in this phase will be the platform upon which objectives are built.

Training Objectives

The final phase in the analysis phase of ID is the writing of training objectives. Training objectives specify the outcomes of training, regardless of content or delivery method. Training objectives have three main functions:

1. to guide the instructional designer in the creation of effective training;
2. as a framework for creating evaluation instruments (written exams, flight tests, and so on);
3. to provide an overview for students, so that they will understand the goals of the training (Morrison et al. 2004).

As discussed in Chapter 4, all learning can be categorized into three domains: cognitive, psychomotor, and affective. Training objectives can be classified into the same three categories, but some training objectives target more than one category simultaneously.

Taxonomy of Cognitive Objectives

Cognitive objectives focus on thought processes targeted by training, such as an understanding of aviation regulations or SOPs. In 1956, a group of measurement specialists led by Benjamin S. Bloom created a framework for classifying cognitive objectives. This classification system, which is commonly referred to in the educational literature as Bloom's Taxonomy, consists of six categories ranging in order from simple to complex: knowledge, comprehension, application, analysis, synthesis, and evaluation (Bloom et al. 1956).

In 2002, David R. Krathwohl revised and expanded upon Bloom's original taxonomy. Krathwohl's cognitive taxonomy comprises the following six components:

1. Remember: the ability to retrieve information from long-term memory, including recognizing and recalling.
2. Understand: the ability to derive the meaning of the material, including interpreting, exemplifying, classifying, summarizing, inferring, comparing, and explaining.
3. Apply: the ability to carry out a procedure within a situation, including executing and implementing.
4. Analyze: the ability to separate information into subparts and understand how they relate to one another, including differentiating, organizing, and attributing.
5. Evaluate: the ability to make judgments based on existing criteria or standards, including checking and critiquing.
6. Create: the ability to generate, plan, produce, or combine individual elements to create a new idea or concept (Krathwohl 2002).

Keep in mind that the complexity of the cognitive process increases throughout the taxonomy, with 'Remember' being the lowest level of learning and 'Create' being the highest. In order for learners to create, they must first have mastered all of the subordinate skills.

Krathwohl's taxonomy is an important element in the design of instructional objectives because it creates perspective and objectivity. For example, if an instructor does not refer to the taxonomy and understand that the task of remembering is the lowest level of learning, he or she may be entirely satisfied with training objectives that are all geared toward memorization. Considering the taxonomy, however, will help the instructor understand how to increase the complexity of cognitive objectives. In addition, use of the taxonomy allows for standardization of both terminology and level of instructional difficulty throughout an organization. Rather than saying simply that a course is easy or difficult, the instructor can specify that the introductory course focuses on remembering and understanding while the advanced course focuses on analyzing, evaluating, and creating. The taxonomy allows this description to be immediately understood by other instructors.

A Psychomotor Taxonomy

The next instructional domain that should be targeted by instructional objectives is the psychomotor. *Psychomotor* refers to hands-on activities, such as how to physically manipulate flight controls to accomplish safe flight. There is no single, widely accepted taxonomy for the psychomotor domain. However, a few researchers have attempted to categorize the progression of psychomotor skills. One such taxonomy orders psychomotor skills according to the degree of coordination required for the task. There are four components of this taxonomy, in increasing order of the level of coordination required:

1. Imitation: the ability to replicate the movements of an action that has been observed:
   - An instructor demonstrates how the control yoke is manipulated to accomplish a maneuver. The student then uses his or her own yoke to replicate the instructor's movement with the yoke, even though he or she is not moving the other coordinating control devices and does not perform the maneuver successfully.
2. Manipulation: the ability to perform a maneuver:
   - With practice, the student is able to move the control yoke to accomplish the flight maneuver with minor airspeed or altitude deviations. The student is still not controlling the coordinating input devices (such as the pedals or throttle).
3. Precision: the ability to accurately perform a maneuver:
   - With continued practice, the student is able to move the control yoke in such a way as to perfectly execute the maneuver. However, the student is still not controlling the coordinating control input devices.
4. Articulation: performs a maneuver in a coordinated manner:
   - Finally, the student is able to move the control yoke to perfectly execute the maneuver. Simultaneously, the student is able to control the other input devices and manage the other onboard devices (Heinich, Molenda and Russell 1992).

Overview of Affective Domain

The affective taxonomy is probably the least understood within aviation training. *Affective* refers to emotional learning associated with flight training, including appropriate attitudes toward safety included in CRM training. Similar to the psychomotor domain, there is not a universally accepted taxonomy that describes the affective domain (Martin and Briggs 1986). However, Martin and Reigeluth (1999) have identified six dimensions of affective development. These six affective dimensions are not a taxonomy, so they do not increase in complexity throughout the list. However, they do offer instructional designers some insights for targeting specific aspects of this domain. The six affective dimensions are:

1. Emotional development: understanding your emotions as well as the emotions of others, and learning to manage emotions.
2. Moral development: establishing personal codes of conduct, often relating to caring, equality, justice, safety, and so on.
3. Social development: developing skills for interacting and building relationships with others.
4. Spiritual development: building an awareness and appreciation for one's soul and a higher religious deity.
5. Aesthetic development: an appreciation for style and beauty and the ability to create it, linked to music and art, as well as the aesthetic of new ideas.
6. Motivational development: developing interests, and the desire to develop new interests—including professional and personal pursuits—because of the pleasure they provide (Martin and Reigeluth 1999).

Writing Instructional Objectives

With a foundational understanding of the three domains of learning—cognitive, psychomotor, and affective—an instructional designer will begin the task of writing instructional objectives. The process of writing learning objectives is based on the task analysis that was completed earlier in the ID process. As an instructional designer, you first write objectives to describe successful performance of each task, and then objectives to describe the skills that a person would need to perform the task, focusing on the skills that learners would not already possess (Mager 1997). Once your objectives have been written, test each one for completeness by asking:

- Does it clearly describe what someone does when achieving the objective?
- Does it describe the conditions that exist while the task is being done?
- Does it define successful performance, such as completion to specifications, completion within a time limit, and so on (Mager 1997)?

The following is an example of an objective for a basic pilot ground school course:

Objective: The learner will be able to complete a visual flight rules (VFR) cross-country flight plan between two airports.

This objective includes both cognitive and psychomotor elements, because learners require not only the knowledge of how to conduct the planning, but also the hands-on skills required to work with their plotter and chart their course of flight on the map.

Associated with each objective will be a set of criteria that define whether the student has successfully achieved the objective. Broadly, the objective will describe what the learner will be able to do after training, while the criteria describe the tools and environment relevant to the task, and how performance is judged (Mager 1997). The following list provides some examples of criteria. It will become clear that key words from the cognitive and psychomotor domains (such as *analyze* and *precisely*) are included within the objectives.

Criteria:

1. Completes all planning within 45 minutes.
2. Uses appropriate tools and reference information, which may include VFR sectional map, plotter, flight computer, and valid weather reports.
3. Correctly analyzes weather reports.
4. Precisely plots course of flight between two airports on map, including 10 nm distance markings.
5. Accurately measures and determines correct true course between two airports.
6. Chooses an appropriate cruise altitude, based on appropriate regulatory and weather information.

As this example illustrates, objectives must be precise and unambiguous. Objectives describe the desired performance of learners after training, not the training content or delivery itself. For example, an objective would not include descriptions of training activities such as 'review course notes on flight planning,' 'attend a 30-minute briefing on weather reports,' or 'work with a fellow student and discuss markings and acronyms on a VFR sectional map.' These statements are not objectives; they refer to activities that an instructional designer may choose to incorporate into training in order to *accomplish* training objectives.

Lastly, it is important to go back to the goal analysis completed earlier in the ID process. The purpose of the goal analysis was to identify characteristics of the professional environment that are important, yet not directly linked to a task (such as professionalism, demeanor, or a safety culture). Before finalizing the list of objectives, an instructional designer should review the goal assessment and incorporate additional training objectives that target organizational goals.

Conclusion

This chapter began with the proverb 'Measure twice, cut once.' Although this proverb is typically associated with construction projects, it is also a helpful consideration within ISD. In construction, the eagerness to complete the job often results in the loss of materials and time, and a lower quality end product. The same can be said for ISD, as the analysis phase is one that people want to rush through or skip altogether. However, the purpose of the analysis is to precisely measure training requirements. Developing training without completing this measurement is likely to result in lost resources and a lower quality of training. This is particularly true within e-learning, especially in the case of asynchronous delivery, which does not allow the instructor to intuitively modify the training in response to immediate feedback from learners. The analysis phase is one of the more time-consuming elements of ISD, and one that is crucial in the creation of effective e-learning.

Practical Summary

- The analysis is the first of five phases in the instructional design (ID) process. The analysis focuses on measuring training requirements through needs, performance, and goal assessments; learner, contextual, and task analyses; and the writing of instructional objectives.
- A needs analysis explores whether training is the best solution to an organizational problem. The needs analysis is an important first step when designing optional training:
  – training that is required, because of regulatory or licensing requirements, should begin with a performance assessment.
- A performance assessment identifies the gap between current performance and ideal performance, and explores whether training is likely to reduce the gap.
- A goal assessment explores characteristics of a professional environment— characteristics that are not directly linked to one's ability to do the job, but are a key determinant in success:
  – for example, a flight instructor may produce several students who successfully complete their flight tests. However, even though the primary professional responsibility was achieved, the instructor may lack the attitude, deportment, and communication skills to be considered a good flight instructor. The goal analysis explores these supplementary factors.
- A learner analysis identifies key characteristics of the student population that might influence learning outcomes, such as age, experience, culture, and gender.
- A contextual analysis analyzes the characteristics of the professional environment that might impact learning outcomes, such as usability, organizational support, scheduling, and transfer context.
- A task analysis is designed to break apart and describe the knowledge, skills, and attitudes required for a job, making the characteristics of expert performance visible and understandable:

- there are five types of task analysis: procedural, learning, cognitive, activity, and subject matter. Each of these is best suited for designing a particular type of learning.
- The final step in the analysis phase of ISD is the writing of training objectives. Training objectives must clearly and unambiguously define the outcomes of training, but not discuss the training process:
  - training objectives are used to guide ID, create evaluation instruments, and provide student guidance.

Chapter 9
Design

Design is not just what it looks like and feels like. Design is how it works.

—Steve Jobs

Overview

Whereas the analysis phase of instructional design (ID) can be considered the foundation of training, the design phase can be likened to the architecture. The design phase can be best understood by the questions that are answered at each step of the process:

- In what order should the training objectives be presented to learners?
    - *Content sequencing* takes the list of training objectives, which have already been developed, and logically organizes them in a way that better facilitates learning:
        - often, the sequence in which a task is conducted in the real world is not the best sequence in which it should be taught.
- How should the training be delivered to learners?
    - The *instructional delivery strategy* reviews the advantages, drawbacks, and development issues associated with synchronous and asynchronous e-learning. In addition, there are situations in which e-learning alone cannot meet the training requirements. Therefore, a strategy for determining the best use of blended learning is presented.
- How can one ensure that the design and types of activities included in e-learning will build the types of skills that the training is meant to produce?
    - Determining which of the *four architectures of e-learning design* is best suited to the type of skill being instructed establishes a strategy for e-learning design. The four architectures define the types of learning activities that should be created.
- What mixture of audio, video, and text-based activities best promotes learning?
    - *Multimedia principles* describe how to maximize learning by using the most efficient combination of media without overloading the learner.
- How can these strategies be used to ensure that the long list of training objectives will be converted into instruction? How can an organization precisely explain to a software developer what the training should do and how it should look?

– The final step in the design process is to build the *course map*. The course map defines how the instruction is organized and how it fits into the larger curriculum. This process leads to the creation of detailed *storyboards*, which are screen-by-screen descriptions of the audio, text, and images required within training. Once completed, these elements clearly define what is required from the software developer.

Introduction

The design phase is where e-learning begins to differ from traditional classroom ID. Some elements of design, such as content sequencing, are important in both e-learning and classroom instructional design. However, the incorporation of e-learning raises new ID questions, such as which delivery method is most appropriate, which learning architecture to use, and how multimedia should be incorporated.

The analysis phase focused on identifying the training need and the objectives that must be accomplished. The design phase moves to the next level: determining the process by which the training objectives will be accomplished.

Content Sequencing

Determining the most appropriate sequence for content to be presented to learners is an important step in the design phase. Yet, there is no simple way to determine the content sequencing. It is important to note that the task analysis and related training objectives are based on the task sequence in the real world. However, this is probably not the best way to sequence instructional content for learners.

Keep in mind that the way training has historically been sequenced is not necessarily ideal. For example, *ab initio* aviation training has historically begun with an introductory flight in an aircraft. However, emerging research suggests that students reach milestones (such as time to solo) more quickly if they pre-train in a flight simulator before setting foot in an aircraft (G. Anderson, personal communication, January 9, 2010). There is nothing novel about training in a flight simulator; however, it is typically included at later stages of training. Changing the *sequence* of instruction to include simulator before aircraft training improves efficiency. Therefore, content sequencing should not be based on how training has always been delivered. Rather, this stage of the design process provides an opportunity to rethink the traditional sequence and identify possible improvements.

Alternatively, for a new training course, there may not be a standard sequence for content delivery. In this situation the sequence may be implied, as you must teach foundational skills (such as takeoffs and landings) before advanced skills (such as precision approaches). However, content sequence is often highly variable, and many sequencing decisions—such as whether to begin a ground school with a lesson on weather or a lesson on air law—are left to the discretion of the instructor or organization. This section will outline some strategies that can be adopted to optimize content sequencing.

Broadly, there are four strategies that can be used to sequence instructional content: world-related, concept, learning, and utilization (developed by Posner and Strike 1976).

World-related sequences are based on the way an item exists in the real world. There are three types of world-related sequences:

1. Space: instructional sequence based on the way an item is physically arranged, including near-to-far, top-to-bottom, and so on:
   - For example, teaching an aircraft walk-around starting with the nose of the aircraft and working around clockwise.
2. Time: instructional sequence based upon when elements occur and the relationships between elements and sub-elements, such as chronological relationships:
   - For example, teaching the early history of aviation starting with the sketches of Leonardo da Vinci in the early 1500s and working up to the Wright brothers' flight in 1903.
3. Physical attributes: instructional sequence based on physical characteristics, such as size, age, or shape:
   - For example, teaching different types of icing accumulation according to shape, such as smooth clear ice and rough rime ice.

Concept-related sequences reflect the way content is sequenced in the real world, focusing on how knowledge is applied in its final form. This sequencing strategy has four subtypes:

1. Class relations: grouping things of the same kind together, teaching broad concepts before details:
   - For example, broadly grouping *ab initio* ground-school topics into categories of air law, meteorology, navigation, and airmanship. Within these categories, broad concepts such as types of clouds will be taught before details such as the flight characteristics a pilot would expect within each cloud type.
2. Propositional relations: organizing instructional content according to the relationships between concepts rather than how the concepts interact with one another in the real world:
   - For example, teaching a theory, such as Newton's first law, before the fact explained by the theory, such as its impact on thrust and drag.
3. Sophistication: organizing instruction according to the level of precision or complexity of the content:
   - For example, teaching Newton's laws before Einstein's Special Theory of Relativity, which is a refinement of Newton's laws.

Learning-related content sequences are based on the psychological understanding of how learning takes place. The argument behind this approach is that the content itself is not as important as the way a human being will process that content.

1. *Empirical prerequisite.* If learning one skill makes it possible to teach a subsequent, more advanced skill, the prerequisite must be sequenced first:
   - For example, a pilot must be taught the skill of landing an aircraft before the skill of conducting a precision approach.
2. *Familiarity.* Considering that internalization of knowledge will be based on an individual's past experiences, familiarity can be used as the basis for content sequencing. This approach presents commonly known concepts before domain-specific concepts.
   - For example, teaching about temperature, which is commonly understood by most people, before teaching the concept of dew point.
3. *Difficulty.* Teach easy concepts before those that are more difficult.
   - For example, teach straight-and-level flight before steep turns.
4. *Interest.* Some concepts within training will be intrinsically interesting. Therefore, instruction should engage the learner by presenting interesting items first.
   - For example, teach the importance of good situation awareness by describing some real-life examples of controlled flight into terrain accidents. Next, teach strategies that can be used to improve a pilot's situation awareness.

Lastly, content can adopt a *utilization-related* sequence, which is based upon how the task is accomplished in the real world.

1. *Procedure.* When a procedure is being taught, it is often logical to teach subtasks in the order they will be completed in the real world:
   - For example, teach each element of a pre-landing check in the order it is presented on the checklist.
2. *Anticipated frequency of utilization.* Teach the concepts that will be used most frequently before concepts that are rarely encountered.
   - For example, in a cold-weather environment, teach about managing aircraft icing before teaching about the risks of dehydration from flying in hot weather.

Learning all of the strategies that can be used to sequence content may seem overwhelming, as it is quite a long list. However, in practice, many of these strategies will be naturally used by most instructors. It is not necessary to memorize the entire list in order to produce good training. Rather, before sequencing the training objectives, review the list of strategies with the goal of identifying new ways of delivering content and ensuring that at least one of the strategies is being incorporated. All too often, instruction is developed in the same sequence in which the training objectives are identified. Thinking creatively about the sequence of instruction can lead to improvements in the quality of training.

The end result of this component of the design phase is a list of training objectives that have been rearranged into a sequence that is appropriate for training. This leads to the next issue, which is how the training will be delivered.

Instructional Delivery Strategy

Several instructional delivery options are available for e-learning. Remember that e-learning is not appropriate or effective for all types of training. The delivery method decision should be based on a systematic review of the strengths and weaknesses of each approach.

Synchronous vs Asynchronous Delivery

The choice between synchronous or asynchronous learning should be based on learner characteristics and training objectives, which were identified in the analysis phase of ID. The advantages, drawbacks, and development issues associated with synchronous and asynchronous e-learning are presented in Table 9.1 overleaf.

Blended Learning

Aviation training is a natural example of blended learning, combining elements of in-aircraft, simulator, and classroom instruction. When the integration of e-learning into an instructional program is being considered, using a blended approach can capitalize on the advantages of both e-learning and classroom instruction. However, as with every component of ID, it is important to follow a systematic decision process instead of guessing which approach would work best.

The best way to determine which delivery methods to choose within a blended learning approach is a four-part process:

1. Consider the sequenced training objectives.
2. For each training objective, make a list of simplified objectives, including the cognitive, psychomotor, and affective elements.
3. For each of the simplified objectives, consider the following:
   - What is the best teaching activity to accomplish this objective?
   - Is human interaction required?
   - How could this instruction be delivered?
4. Then, list the objectives according to which activities should be accomplished before classroom training, which activities require human interaction, and which activities can be delivered on-the-line once learners return to the job. These three components illustrate the blended learning delivery strategy:

Table 9.1 Synchronous vs. asynchronous e-learning

	Advantages	Drawbacks	Development
Synchronous	• Allows instructors to train several classrooms simultaneously • Allows for lengthy discussions with instructor and peers • Can improve extrinsic motivation, through peer pressure • Can incorporate several types of media (video, slideshows, etc.) • Training is not limited by geographic location • No travel expenses	• Can become confusing and time-consuming with a large number of participants • Instruction must be carefully designed and controlled to avoid discussions going off-topic • Facilitator must be trained to coordinate participants and deliver instruction effectively • Ill-suited for participants who have different training needs (novices vs. experts) • Logistically difficult for learners in different time zones	• Can use existing hardware (telephone, computer with Internet connection) or specialized hardware (webcam, computer headset, and microphone) • Can use existing software (online meeting programs) or specialized synchronous e-learning programs • Material should be distributed in advance, to allow for learner preparation and organization • Requires 25–40 hours of development for every one hour of instruction
Asynchronous	• Can be adaptive • Can be self-paced • Can track performance and maintain company-wide training database • Can be designed to appeal to different learners (auditory, visual, tactile) • Can reduce content ambiguity, because content is stable • Can provide immediate feedback • Can incorporate simulation • Great option for learners with highly variable work schedules that make predetermined meeting times a challenge	• Ineffective for lengthy text-based material • Can be boring • Can be prohibitively expensive • Requires skilled software developers, typically contracted	• Development costs vary, according to complexity of graphics and interactions, ranging from $15,000 to $35,000 per hour of finished training program (costs will be lower if organizations complete ID in-house) • 50–400 hours of development for every one hour of completed training (depending on the number of interactions and type of design)

Source: Adapted from Horton 2006 and Piskurich 2006.

a. pre-learning (e-learning);
b. training center (classroom and simulator);
c. on-the-line (e-learning or m-learning).

Example of blended learning decision process An important component of crew resource management (CRM) training is effective communication. Simplified objectives for this aspect of training may include the following:

- Cognitive:
    1. Identify examples of good and bad flight deck communication.
    2. Understand types of leadership styles.
    3. Be able to recite 3–4 examples of accidents caused by poor communication.
- Psychomotor:
    1. Interact effectively with crewmate on the flight deck.
- Affective:
    1. Desire good communication with crewmembers.

For each of the sample objectives, there are several considerations. First, what experience is likely to produce the best learning? This decision should be based on knowledge of the learners as well as expertise in the subject area, so current instructors are the ideal group with whom to work through this process. The following are examples of how the above objectives could be addressed:

1. Identification of good and bad examples of communication is probably best accomplished by gathering a group of pilots together and guiding a discussion and thinking activity. This may occur in a brick-and-mortar classroom or through e-learning.
2. Memorization of leadership styles is probably best accomplished through private reading and practices, delivered either electronically or through use of books.
3. Recitation of poor communication accidents requires private reading. The text should be presented in a case-based format. This activity could be delivered on paper or electronically.
4. The ability to interact effectively with a crewmate is probably best addressed through role-playing activities conducted in a flight simulator with a crewmate and observed by a flight instructor. However, role playing in a classroom or e-learning environment may also be effective.
5. The desire for good communication may be fostered through instructor storytelling. This is likely best accomplished in a face-to-face (F2F) classroom setting but is also feasible through e-learning.

This process is presented in Table 9.2.

Table 9.2　Analysis of training objectives for blended learning

Objective	Best Way to Teach	Human Interaction Required?	Delivery Method
1. Identify examples of good and bad communication	Thinking activity, group discussion	1st choice: F2F with instructor and peers 2nd choice: synchronous e-learning	Classroom or synchronous e-learning
2. Understand leadership styles	Readings: memorize and practice	Not required	Book or e-learning
3. Recite examples of poor communication accidents	Case studies: memorize and practice	Not required	Book or e-learning
4. Interact effectively with crewmate	Role playing, practice	1st choice: F2F with partner observed by instructor 2nd choice: synchronous e-learning with virtual partner observed by instructor	1st choice: flight simulator 2nd choice: Classroom 3rd choice: e-learning
5. Desire for good communication	Storytelling	1st choice: F2F with instructor 2nd choice: synchronous e-learning with instructor 3rd choice: asynchronous with virtual coach	1st choice: classroom 2nd choice: synchronous e-learning 3rd choice: asynchronous e-learning

Source: Adapted from Horton 2006.

Clearly, there are a number of ways to accomplish the overall goal of improving communication. Several factors play a part in choosing among delivery methods. Sometimes instructional delivery decisions are guided by organizational factors—such as a company's training budget or an organizational culture that strives to be on the cutting edge of technology—rather than by the ID itself. Generally, however, training should be designed to create maximum learning with minimum cost. One strategy is to conduct all training that does not require F2F interaction through e-learning, thereby minimizing not only instructor and classroom resources but also each learner's time at the training center off-the-line (Horton 2006).

Horton (2006) suggests a 'sandwich' strategy for blended learning, in which e-learning elements are scheduled before and after classroom instruction. This strategy has been adapted for aviation companies to create the pre-training, training center, on-the-line blended learning model. *Pre-training* is presented through e-learning. Pre-training is meant to deliver the foundational knowledge and skills that learners require before classroom and simulator instruction. *Training center* learning is classroom and simulator-based instruction, specifically for topics that require human and aircraft-equipment interaction. *On-the-line* learning is accomplished through e-learning or m-learning. On-the-line learning extends training beyond the classroom to the workplace. The purpose of on-the-line learning is to build on what was learned at the training center (for example, to refresh each learner's memory of concepts, distribute relevant cases or practice activities, or evaluate performance to track learning decay over time, and so on).

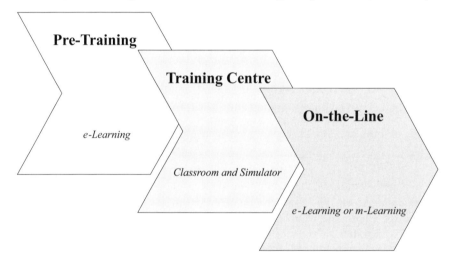

Figure 9.1   A blended learning strategy for aviation training

Applying this strategy to the CRM communication example:

- Pre-training via e-learning:
  – Objectives 2 and 3 (Understand leadership styles and Recite examples of accidents associated with poor communication).
- Training Center via classroom and simulator:
  – Objectives 1 and 4 (Memorize leadership styles and Interact with crewmate) would be accomplished at the training center, the first in a classroom setting and the latter in a flight simulator.

- On-the-line:
  - Objective 5 (Desire good communication) would be completed on-the-line through asynchronous e-learning.

This strategy recognizes that not all training is feasible over the Internet. e-Learning cannot and will not replace all classroom and simulator instruction. However, this strategy separates out the aspects of training that do not require human interaction and therefore can and should be delivered online to maximize efficiency while minimizing costs. In addition, the on-the-line portion of training allows instruction to be customized, allowing each individual learner to reach his or her maximum potential beyond the minimum performance standard.

The Four Architectures of e-Learning Design

For the aspects of training that will be delivered via e-learning, it is crucial to consider, before creating the instruction, whether the skills to be conveyed to learners are classified as near-transfer or far-transfer skills (Clark 2000). Near-transfer skills, such as setting a frequency on an aircraft radio, are performed the same way each time. By comparison, far-transfer tasks require several adaptations each time they are performed. For example, landing an aircraft is a far-transfer task, because for every landing an individual must consider weather, runway conditions, and traffic, all of which are highly variable. Instruction for far-transfer tasks requires learners to think at a higher level of complexity than for near-transfer skills.

The type of skill to be taught is important, because it influences which training architecture will be ideal. There are four training architectures: receptive, behavioral, guided discovery, and exploratory (Clark 2000). The architecture chosen for a particular course impacts the design and activities included in the e-learning program. There are strengths and weaknesses associated with each approach. However, e-learning can incorporate aspects of several architectures, capitalizing on the strengths of each one.

Every individual who has sat in a classroom has experienced a *receptive architecture*. As Clark (2000) describes, this is the most ancient and, unfortunately, most popular classroom-based training methodology. The perspective behind this approach is that learners are like sponges that can soak up knowledge when exposed to it through a lecture, reading a textbook, or watching a non-interactive video. The most important identifying feature of a receptive architecture is that there is no, or very little, interaction. The instructor controls the sequence and content of information and the rate of delivery. The challenges of a receptive architecture are twofold. First, it may result in cognitive overload, as students cannot slow down the pace of information when they become overwhelmed. It can also result in failure to encode the information in long-term memory (LTM), as an instructor may have difficulty relating the information to the learners' past experience in a way that makes sense to them. Overall, learners must be motivated and have good learning skills to effectively learn in a receptive environment. The receptive architecture method is useful for delivering information, such as in a preflight briefing, but not for building skills (Clark 2000).

A *behavioral architecture* is one of the most popular e-learning architectures, and is widely considered a tried-and-true approach. This methodology takes the perspective that learning occurs through slowly building skills from simple to complex, requiring the learner to interact and correctly respond to carefully designed activities within the training program. This approach is characterized by short lessons that build upon each other, frequent incorporation of interactive exercises, and providing feedback to inform learners of their progress. The behavioral architecture approach manages cognitive load by allowing learners to self-pace instruction, and it encourages LTM encoding through frequent opportunities for interaction with activities and exercises. This methodology is useful in the development of near-transfer skills, but may not be the best strategy for far-transfer skills. In addition, expert learners may perform poorly, experiencing an expertise reversal effect, as they may find the approach to be too descriptive and lengthy (Clark 2000). Therefore, a behavioral architecture is recommended for novices and for the instruction of near-transfer skills.

The *guided discovery architecture* is based on constructivist learning principles. In guided discovery, the role of instruction is to provide information or experiences that allow learners to link new information to that which is already held within their LTM. Therefore, the knowledge produced through guided discovery courses will be uniquely constructed by each individual rather than memorized by rote. A case-based approach is a common method of designing guided discovery learning, particularly in business learning. There are no right or wrong answers within this approach, and feedback is provided from multiple sources. For example, if a pilot is asked to operate a computer-based flight simulator within a scenario, feedback could be incorporated through communication with a computer-generated captain character, reminder radio calls from air traffic control, a clock that presents time for comparison with estimated time en route (ETE) calculations, and an online expert instructor (either live or computer-generated) who debriefs the pilot-learner at the conclusion of the scenario. In guided-discovery architecture, learning is based in the real world, with realistic challenges and opportunities, and the learner has a high level of control and access to resources. This approach may cause cognitive overload in novice learners. However, it should facilitate LTM encoding, as it is highly interactive and requires independent thought. If the expertise levels of learners vary significantly, a supporting behavioral course can be included to allow novices to gain the knowledge required to interact with the guided discovery course. Overall, this approach is ideal for the development of far-transfer problem-solving skills in experienced learners (Clark 2000).

Last is the *exploratory architecture*. The foundation of this approach is a very high level of learner control. Conducting research over the Internet is an example of an exploratory architecture. Learners have access to a large amount of information, and it is up to the learner to know which information is important and to possess the background knowledge necessary to understand it. e-Learning courses that are based on this architecture should be considered a database, tool, or resource that learners can sort through as they choose. A major shortcoming of this approach is that learners may become disoriented by massive amounts of information, unless effective navigation tools are incorporated. An example of such a navigation tool is a left-hand menu frame that allows learners to return to a specific topic at any time. If learner characteristics vary, instructional information should be organized in small lessons and sequenced from simple to complex. This provides the structure that novices need, and allows experts to skip ahead to locate the information they want (Clark 2000).

Cognitive Apprenticeships

An example of a guided discovery approach to e-learning is the cognitive apprenticeship. In Chapter 4, a cognitive apprenticeship was presented as a logical fit within the aviation industry. This approach makes sense in aviation, because pilot training has traditionally been conducted according to an apprenticeship model. Cognitive apprenticeships take the historical understanding of apprenticeship to a new level, making the cognitive processes of experts visible to learners. In this manner, learners can observe not just the psychomotor actions of an instructor, but also what the instructor is thinking about and paying attention to while completing a task.

To assist in the design of a cognitive apprenticeship course, Collins, Brown and Newman (1989) present four dimensions of the ideal learning environment: content, methods, sequence, and sociology:

- *Content*. The material within this type of course focuses on domain knowledge as well as heuristic, control, and learning strategies. In aviation, *content* refers not only to the aviation-specific knowledge required to operate within the environment, but also to problem-solving 'tricks of the trade' strategies, guidance in how to choose appropriate problem-solving strategies and manage complex situations, and strategies for learning and seeking out new knowledge when necessary.
- *Methods*. These are the techniques that can be used to help learners observe and develop the skills of experts. Examples include modeling, coaching, scaffolding and fading, articulation, reflection, and exploration. Ultimately, the goal of using appropriate methods is to 'give students the opportunity to observe, engage in, and invent or discover expert strategies in context' (Collins, Brown and Newman 1989: 481).
- *Sequence*. This is an important consideration, as it facilitates the development of expert skills and an understanding of when and where the skills can be applied to real-world settings. Sequencing is accomplished through gradually increasing the complexity and diversity of scenarios,

while teaching students to understand the 'big picture' of the situation before focusing on details.
- *Sociology*. Also known as *situated learning*, the sociological aspect refers to the integration of real-world characteristics (culture, technological, and social) within the learning environment. As learners will be working cooperatively with other people in the real world, it is helpful to incorporate cooperative problem solving, which increases motivation and enhances learning. Intrinsic motivation should be fostered through the creation of learning that is interesting and relevant to learners, as opposed to forcing the learners through a monotonous training program with the extrinsic motivation of passing a course upon completion. Lastly, training can exploit competition by giving multiple students identical scenarios and having them compare their results. Such comparison encourages improvement because it highlights strengths and weaknesses; however, it can be intimidating for some learners and must be designed carefully.

Multimedia Principles

Before creating an e-learning course, it is important to understand how multimedia can be effectively integrated into instruction. The reality is that skilled incorporation of multimedia enhances learning, while poor integration of multimedia hurts learning. An understanding of these principles is necessary even for aviation companies that plan to contract a software development company to develop their e-learning. It is extremely important for management to recognize the differences between good and bad e-learning design, no matter whether the instruction will be developed in-house or by outsiders.

Multimedia refers to the combination of various types of electronic media, such as video, audio, graphics, and pictures. Clark and Mayer (2008), on the basis of scientific research, suggest seven multimedia principles that are used in combination to maximize the quality of e-learning:

1. *The multimedia principle* (use both words and pictures). It is recommended that e-learning present a combination of words (text or auditory) and pictures (graphs, pictures, animations, videos, and so on). Combination results in better learning, because connecting the words to the pictures facilitates the processing of information.
2. *The contiguity principle* (keep the words and corresponding pictures close together). Don't make learners scroll to the bottom of a page to view a graph related to the text they're reading. Integrating words and corresponding pictures reduces the cognitive load by not requiring learners to remember the words while visually searching for the picture. Also, auditory words should be presented simultaneously with the pictures they describe. After an on-screen evaluation, feedback should pop up on the same screen beside

the original question and the learner's response, so that the learner can compare the feedback to the question and answer.
3. *The modality principle* (use audio instead of written text). In multimedia learning, presenting words as audio improves learning because the information is distributed across the two channels of working memory: auditory (for words) and visual (for pictures). Auditory words are best for descriptions, although text remains the best option for information that must be referenced.
4. *The redundancy principle* (explain pictures with an auditory description, or as on-screen text, not both). Redundant textual descriptions, replicating the audio narration with on-screen text, should be avoided, because learners will pay too much attention to the words and ignore the pictures.
5. *The coherence principle* (eliminate any material that does not relate to a training objective). Often e-learning incorporates unrelated music, examples, or stories to motivate learners. These interesting tidbits distract learners from the instructional objectives and should be deleted.
6. *The personalization principle* (relate to learners by using a conversational tone and on-screen coach characters). Using a coach character and a natural conversational tone (rather than formal language) encourages learners to 'engage with the computer as a social conversational partner' (Clark and Mayer 2008: 158).
7. *The segmentation and pretraining principles* (break apart training into manageable chunks). To avoid overloading the learner with material, break instruction into small parts and provide pre-training on foundational concepts.

Building the Course Map

At this point in the design process, the designer has a clear understanding of what needs to be taught (list of objectives); the order of instruction (content sequence); how training will be delivered (synchronous, asynchronous, or blended learning); a broad design strategy that targets the type of skill required (four architectures); and an understanding of how to use multimedia effectively. The next step is where all of the analysis and planning pays off: building the course map and storyboarding.

All instruction will be developed within five broad categories of instruction: curriculum, course, lesson, module, and learning activities.

- *Curriculum.* This is the broadest category of instruction, and refers to a complete program of study:
  - an example of a curriculum is the training required for a commercial pilot's license.
- *Course.* Within each curriculum will be several courses. A course is a broad grouping of instructional content:

- an example of a course is the meteorology portion of ground school instruction.
- *Lesson*. Within each course there will be several lessons. Typically, lessons will be spread out over several weeks or months, with each lesson focusing on a specific section of the course:
  - for example, a meteorology lesson may focus on weather fronts.
- *Module*. To accomplish the goals of a lesson, several modules will be developed. Each module focuses on an aspect of the lesson:
  - for example, within the weather front lesson, there would be several modules, including cold front, warm front, and occluded front.
- *Learning activities*. A learning activity is something that a learner interacts with while learning a chunk of instruction. Each learning activity is created by a specialist and can be assembled in flexible and unique ways to accomplish training objectives. In this regard, learning activities are building blocks that can be combined in limitless ways:
  - examples of learning activities within the cold front module may include a computer-based cross-section of a cold front, text-based descriptions of cold fronts followed by a quiz, or a weather report and a map that a learner must analyze and interpret to appropriately overlay a cold front symbol.

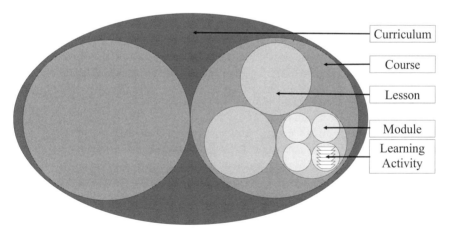

Figure 9.2   Overview of the instructional hierarchy

Learning activities should be strategically organized within each module. Mager (1997) suggests organizing the module in the following manner (see also Figure 9.3):

1. Each module should begin with an overview of how this section of training fits into the larger curriculum.

2. Next, the module should clearly define the training objective that it is targeting. Clearly stating the objective allows learners to understand the goal of the module.
3. When required (for example, for a hands-on psychomotor objective), the training should then describe the skill that learners must attain in order to master the objective.
4. The module should then describe why meeting this objective is important to learners. This step is meant to solicit buy-in, promoting intrinsic motivation to successfully complete training.
5. When necessary, the training program should present a visual demonstration of the movements required to attain the objective.
6. The training program will then deliver the instruction. The purpose of this part of the training is to convey the appropriate knowledge, skill, or attitude required for the training objective. The variety of learning activities included in this portion of a module is limited only by the designer's imagination. However, one must always remember to choose learning activities that will accomplish the module's training objective.
7. The module must then incorporate a method of practice, to allow learners to practice applying the new knowledge, skill, or ability. Descriptive feedback should be provided to allow learners to compare their performance against the ideal.
8. When required, incorporate a self-check to allow learners to determine whether their level of skill meets the requirements for the training objective.

To begin mapping the course, create a flow chart beginning with the curriculum and flowing down through the courses, lessons, modules, and instructional objectives. Once these organizational concepts have been identified, and each module has been organized according to the process in Figure 9.3, the process of converting instructional objectives into learning activities begins. There are many different types of learning activities that can be incorporated into training. A list of learning activities is presented in Table 9.3.

When developing asynchronous e-learning, a greater level of precision is required within the course map. Broad instructional strategies within each module must be converted into precise, step-by-step learning activities, which are typically created within storyboards.

Storyboarding

A storyboard is a visual plan for an e-learning program, which clearly lays out the instructional, design, and interactive elements screen-by-screen. To create learning activities for each instructional objective, storyboards are created to describe the audio, text, images or interactivity, and branching. Branching, another term for adaptive instruction, refers to training that is not delivered linearly but that becomes more difficult or less difficult, depending on learner responses.

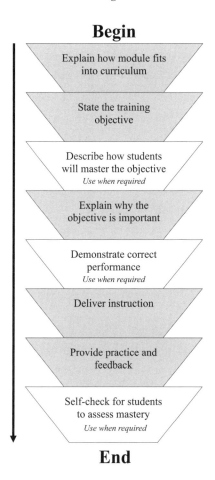

Figure 9.3 **The organization of modules (adapted from Mager 1997)**

A word of caution: If an organization plans to contract an e-learning development company rather than develop e-learning in-house, it is wise to consult the company before storyboarding takes place, as the cost of development increases significantly with the number of interactions included in the instruction. In addition, the types of learning activities may be limited by the skills and technology of the development group. Advice on choosing a reputable e-learning developer is presented in Chapter 10.

Broadly, there are four steps in the storyboarding process (Figure 9.4 presents an example of a completed storyboard template):

1. First, describe the overarching design characteristics of the training program:
    - What font and colors are appropriate, given the culture of the industry and the learner analysis?

Table 9.3   Examples of training activities

Types of Activities	Description
Articulation	Learners are asked to write out their thoughts, for analysis purposes and to compare their internal definitions with classmates.
Behavior Modeling	Effective behaviors are demonstrated for learners, with each aspect of the behavior described in detail. This approach may be useful for nontechnical skills.
Case Study	A description of a situation is presented to learners for analysis purposes. Aviation accidents are commonly analyzed using a case study approach.
Coaching	Learners are provided with feedback from an expert. With a student and flight instructor, coaching is a common and natural strategy within aviation training. Through e-learning, coaching can be accomplished through an animated coach character.
Committee	The group of learners is segregated into small groups, each of which is asked to solve an aspect of the problem. Following discussion, the class reconvenes to discuss their solutions.
Critique	Learners are asked to critically analyze a situation and present their findings and opinions.
Debate	A group of learners is broken into two groups, each of which takes an opposing side of an argument.
Demonstration	An expert demonstrates a task for learners.
Discussion	Conversation between learners and with an instructor. Should be structured toward the training objective. Can be conducted live through voice communication, or asynchronously through message boards.
Discovery Activities	Allow learners to explore and experiment with an electronic medium, with the goal of independently finding the answer to a problem.
Drill	A series of practice activities that are designed to improve performance and retention.
Guided Mental Practice	Learners watch a video and are asked to imagine themselves interacting with the elements in the video.
Instruments	Lists that are completed by learners to provide some insight about themselves or a topic, such as checklists or questionnaires.

Table 9.3   Examples of training activities *continued*

Types of Activities	Description
Internet Research	Learners are given a problem and asked to search for the answer online.
Interaction	This term refers to a broad range of activities that require the learner to interact with another learner, the training material, or the instructor.
Interview	Learners have the ability to ask questions of an expert, either in person or electronically.
Job Aids	Tools that are given to learners to help them do their jobs, such as an in-flight checklist.
Laboratory	An area where learners are given the tools and equipment to practice applying concepts or techniques. For example, a laboratory could be created electronically to allow students to experiment with weather systems or flight dynamics.
Lecture	An oral presentation that typically does not include interactive activities.
Mental Practice	Learners quietly imagine an activity, with the purpose of improving performance.
Modeling	Learners are presented with an example of expert performance and are asked to mimic the knowledge, skills, and attitudes.
Panel	Learners observe a discussion by a group of experts.
Quiz	Learners are asked to answer a series of questions. Often used to assess learning.
Readings	Text-based material that learners are asked to review.
Reflection	After an activity or presentation, learners are asked to write out their thoughts, opinions, and understanding of the material.
Role Play	Learners are placed in a situation where they act out a role, such as pilot, flight attendant, or air traffic controller.
Scaffolding and Fading	Learners are presented with very detailed guidance about how to perform a task. With practice, the guidance fades, until the learner is completing the task independently with no guidance.

Table 9.3   Examples of training activities *concluded*

Types of Activities	Description
Simulation	A recreation of real-world flight conditions, allowing learners to practice in-flight activities without the cost or risk of flight training.
Storytelling	An instructor, either live or automated, tells the learner about a personal experience that is relevant to the training objective.
Thinking Activity	Learners are presented with a situation and asked to critically analyze it and identify strengths and weaknesses.
Virtual Field Trip	Instead of visiting a historically significant location in person, a video or digital recreation of the scene is presented to the learner.
Whiteboards	A software application, usually within a learning management system, that allows learners to connect online with a group of peers. Whiteboards feature the ability to sketch pictures as needed. Often used for visual brainstorming sessions.
Worked Example	Instead of being given just the answer to a problem, learners are presented with the process through which that answer was found. For example, when teaching flight planning, instructors present the navigation calculations step-by-step until the correct answer is found, instead of just showing students a completed flight plan with the answers.

Source: Portions adapted from Piskurich 2006.

- If a coach character is being used, should it be male or female, how old should it look, how should it be dressed, what race should it be?
    - Generally, the coach character should look like the learners.
    - With a diverse group of learners, the most popular racial design of animated characters is Polynesian. e-Learning developers use Polynesian-looking characters because they have physical characteristics that are similar, and therefore relatable, to many different races.
- What navigational elements and reference materials are required?
    - Navigational elements may include Rewind, Play/Pause, Fast forward, and Return to main menu buttons.
    - Reference materials may include a glossary, flight manual, map, or dictionary.
2. A decision must be made whether to use commercial storyboarding software or to simply create a storyboard template within a word processing program

Curriculum	Single-Pilot Resource Management (SRM)		
Course	Introduction to SRM		
Lesson	Benefits of SRM		
Module	Manage Congested Skies		
Training Objective	Understand that increase in air traffic and introduction of Technically Advanced Aircraft (TAA) and Very Light Jets (VLJs) will lead to airspace congestion		
Screen	3 of 5		
Audio		**Screen Text**	**Image/Interactivity**
Another key benefit that SRM training provides is that it helps pilots manage congested skies.		SRM Training ✶ Manage Congested Skies	Image request – show image of many planes in the sky
That is, it will help you maintain awareness of other aircraft and manage the increased workload, even as air traffic increases.			Interactivity request – Animate a safe flight path for one of the planes in the image above
For instance, air traffic is expected to increase dramatically by 2025. Do you know by how much?		How much is air traffic expected to increase in 2025? 500% 300% 100% 50%	Interactivity request – multiple choice question – the correct answer is 300%
This will result in general aviation (GA) pilots flying in much more heavily-congested airspace.		How much is air traffic expected to increase in 2025? 500% 300% 100% 50%	Interactivity request – place a check mark beside 300% and ensure the learner's answer is visible
With technically advanced aircraft and very light jets on the horizon, GA pilots will be flying more technologically advanced aircraft, at faster speeds, and higher altitudes than previously available. SRM training will help ensure you are prepared to deal with the future state of the aviation industry.			Image request – show images of technically advanced aircraft and light jets
Branching			
Notes			

Figure 9.4   Storyboard

(as shown in Figure 9.4). There are many commercial storyboarding tools on the market. If creating a storyboard template, include the following characteristics:
- Headings:
  - curriculum
  - course
  - lesson
  - module
  - training objective(s) for that module
  - screen number:
    - each storyboard represents one screen, and therefore each storyboard should identify the screen number. Screens should be labeled sequentially.
- Description of learning activities, using three columns:
  - audio
  - text
  - image or interactive elements.
- Notes:
  - branching:
    - describing any adaptive elements of the training program.
  - general notes.

3. Next is the lengthy process of completing all of the storyboards for a training program. The best way to do this is to start at the top of the storyboards with the headings. Then, work down to complete the audio, text, image or interactive aspects, branching, and notes.
   - The audio should include a complete script, along with any music or sound effects that are included on the screen.
   - The text should include precise descriptions of words, along with their position onscreen.
   - The image/interactive area should describe or show pictures, videos, simulations, and activities.
   - The branching section should describe how the training adapts to the learners' response (for example, when a learner responds correctly or quickly skips ahead to a different storyboard).
   - The final section is for notes, where any additional notes to the developer can be included.
4. Last is the review process. All storyboards should be reviewed, preferably by someone who was not directly involved in their creation (such as another training manager or an expert in the field), to ensure that the learning activities directly address the training objectives. A revised flow chart should be created, reflecting the final organization and structure of training.

The final product of this process is a complete set of storyboards that precisely describe the design, interactivity, and content of training. Typically, this phase of the ID process is contracted out to a developer. However, if storyboarding can be completed in-house, it is likely to result in significant cost savings and a program that is more closely aligned to the needs and culture of the organization.

Conclusion

The purpose of the design component of ID is to transform training objectives into a precise page-by-page storyboard that describes the instructional content. However, many things must be considered in order to get to this point, such as the most appropriate sequence for content, the delivery method, the foundational learning architecture, and multimedia principles. The creation of precise storyboards ensures that the training content targets key objectives, and that the final product created in the development phase will have the design, information, and interactivity that were originally envisioned.

Practical Summary

- Training should not necessarily be delivered in the order in which training objectives were identified.
    - Several approaches can be used to strategically sequence content, such as how a task is performed sequentially, the level of complexity or sophistication, the level of interest or familiarity, or how often the task is used in the real world.
    - While designing the training, it is not necessary to have all of these approaches memorized. Just refer to them and put some careful thought into the order in which instruction will be delivered to students.
- Several delivery options are available for training. e-learning is not an appropriate way to accomplish every training objective. Some objectives are best accomplished with face-to-face (F2F) interaction.
- A blended learning approach can be used to maximize the efficiency of training while minimizing costs. This approach involves using e-learning whenever F2F interaction is not required:
    - A blended learning strategy (pre-training, training center, on-the-line) was presented in this chapter. In this model, foundational skills are delivered via e-learning before pilots come to the training center. Classroom and simulator instruction is accomplished F2F while pilots are off-the-line at the training center. Once they return on-the-line, training is extended to the real world through follow-up exercises delivered via e-learning or m-learning.
- Before building an e-learning course, one must consider the type of skill that the training is meant to produce. Depending on the type of skill required, a learning architecture must be chosen. Each architecture suggests a strategy

for the activities that should be used to accomplish training objectives. Several architectures may be integrated within a single course:
- receptive architecture exposes learners to information (for example, in lecture format) and expects them to 'soak it up';
- behavioral architecture, which is commonly used in e-learning, builds skills from simple to complex through interactive training activities;
- guided discovery architecture (for example, cognitive apprenticeship) provides experiences and situations that learners interact with, allowing them to discover the answers to their questions independently;
- exploratory architecture (exemplified by researching over the Internet) provides an enormous amount of information and allows learners to work through it completely on their own.

- There are seven multimedia principles, based on scientific research, that suggest the most appropriate way to present pictures, audio, and text:
  1. use both words and pictures;
  2. keep words and corresponding pictures close together;
  3. when possible, use audio instead of written text;
  4. explain pictures with an auditory description, or (as a second option) on-screen text, but not both;
  5. eliminate any material that is interesting but does not relate to a training objective;
  6. relate to learners by using a conversational tone and on-screen coach characters;
  7. break apart training into manageable chunks.
- Next, the process of building the course map begins. There are five levels of instruction, the most broad being curriculum, and becoming more specific through course, lesson, module, and learning activity:
  - each module should be organized in a specific way to target training objectives:
    1. explain how the module fits into curriculum;
    2. state the training objective;
    3. describe how students will master the objective;
    4. explain why the objective is important;
    5. demonstrate correct performance;
    6. deliver instruction;
    7. provide practice and feedback;
    8. self-check for students to assess mastery of skill.
  - Next, precise page-by-page storyboards should be created to describe the audio, text, images or interactivity, and branching elements of the training program.

Chapter 10
Development

I never teach my pupils;
I only attempt to provide the conditions in which they can learn.

—Albert Einstein

Overview

The purpose of this chapter is to familiarize the reader with the development phase of instructional design (ID). This will be accomplished by reviewing:

- The roles that are involved in in-house development of e-learning.
- Considerations for choosing an external e-learning development company:
  - how to write an e-learning request for proposal (RFP).
- The e-learning development process:
  - choice of interface:
    - learning portals
    - learning management systems
    - web-based delivery.
  - role of authoring tools;
  - importance of considering bandwidth;
  - an overview of the stages of production:
    - rapid prototyping
    - alpha testing
    - beta testing.

Introduction

The best way to understand the development phase of ID is to visualize what the end product will be. The development phase transforms the course map into a fully functional instructional unit that is ready to implement within an organization. Unlike the analysis and design phases, which incorporate a lot of theory, the development phase of ID is very practical, with a strong focus on project management.

Developing e-Learning In-House

Developing a custom e-learning program may be prohibitively expensive for many organizations. However, for those companies that choose to develop their own e-learning, there are several roles that must be filled. These are described in the following paragraphs (adapted from Kruse 2002).

Project Manager

The role of the project manager is to organize how and when tasks will be accomplished, to coordinate all team members to accomplish those tasks, to communicate the project status to decision-makers through progress reports, and to ensure that the finished product is completed on time and on budget. The project manager has responsibility over all other team members, with the exception of the management team that sponsors the project.

Subject Matter Expert (SME)

The subject matter expert (SME) is a designated person within the company who contributes his or her expertise to the project. The SME's expertise must be context specific, meaning that if you are developing training for pilots, the SME should be a master pilot with a very high level of seniority. The role of the SME is to educate the rest of the development team about the industry. The SME will ensure that the training is suitable to the culture, procedures, and rules of thumb of the organization. This person will review storyboards, scripts, and e-learning prototypes for suitability.

Instructional Designer

The role of the instructional designer is to conduct the task analysis, identify training objectives, map the course, and create detailed storyboards. The instructional designer must have an understanding of how to use technology appropriately to accomplish training goals. The instructional designer will work closely with the writer, SME, and programmer.

Writer

Building upon the storyboards developed by the instructional designer, the writer refines the audio script and screen text for language and clarity. In addition, the writer will work with the programmer and graphic artist to collectively create the training interface design.

Software Programmer

Programmers use various authoring systems and/or programming languages to develop e-learning. The programmer is not responsible for ID decisions and must therefore follow the course map and storyboards precisely. The programmer will create the alpha and beta versions of the training program, and debug as necessary. In the case of medium to large organizations, the software programmer might also create a data management system that interfaces with the learning management system (LMS) to track student progress.

Graphic Artist

An e-learning course features many artistic elements. Artistic decisions must be made regarding the look of control buttons, menus, screen layouts, graphics, and interactive elements. These artistic elements are typically created by a graphic artist. Ultimately, the graphic artist's role is to creatively convert the textual descriptions in the storyboards into attractive images. Graphic artists must understand multimedia principles and human–computer interaction.

Video and Audio Producers

Occasionally, videos can be purchased and incorporated into training. However, more often than not, original videos must be created for instruction. In addition, all of the audio dialogue required for training must be collected. This process involves casting voice and acting talent; organizing the production by setting up shoots and studio time; and post-production, including editing and quality assurance of audio and video elements. This aspect of development is typically subcontracted, even when training is built in-house.

Reviewers

Once a version of the training program has been completed, it should be distributed to people who are not members of the development team; these people will be asked to review the program for clarity and thoroughness. Several types of reviewers should be chosen, to reflect the student and instructor population. In addition, someone with strong editing skills should review the training to carefully check for language and sequencing errors. Reviewers should be asked to complete a training review form, where descriptions of bugs and suggestions for improvement can be written out in a page-by-page format.

Choosing an External e-Learning Development Company

It is unlikely that most aviation companies will have the capacity to develop their own e-learning in-house. Most companies, once they have completed the analysis and design phases of ID, are likely to contract an e-learning developer. If development costs are prohibitively expensive, and the training is not unique to a specific organization, consider partnering with other aviation companies to share development costs.

Before beginning the process of choosing a vendor, keep in mind that e-learning developers have a reputation for aggressively pursuing potential clients. This is not necessarily a bad thing, as sales are a necessary component of a successful company. However, to avoid becoming bombarded with pamphlets and sales calls, it is helpful to have a clear RFP and some insight about what to look for in a reputable e-learning development company.

In a perfect world, an aviation company would be able to trust a developer to produce a good product based on sound multimedia principles. However, this is not always the case. There is a wide range in the quality of e-learning developers, including some who produce excellent e-learning on time, developed according to sound multimedia and ID principles; and some fly-by-night operations whose courses are little more than repurposed PowerPoint presentations and who drag on delivery, requiring the unsuspecting company to supply more and more cash for an inferior product.

To increase your chances of contracting a reliable e-learning developer, consider the following points:

- *Visit their facility*. Can you see a team of software developers at work on various projects? Does the developer maintain full-time staff? Fly-by-night operations may rely primarily on contract-based staff, who will only be contracted when there is money in hand.
- *Past work*. Does the e-learning developer have a long list of past clients? Will they allow you to review courses developed for others? When you review past courses, what is your impression of their quality (based on your understanding of ID)? What is their track record for meeting deadlines for past clients?
- *Reputation*. How long have they been in business? Do they have a history and reputation in the industry?
- *Project management*. Do they employ professionals with project management experience? As a client, will you know the name of the project manager handling your case?
- *Licensing*. Is there a legal obligation to pay the developer each time the course is delivered to a student? Who owns the intellectual property? Typically, when customized e-learning is developed and paid for, it becomes the full property of the aviation company, rather than the developer. Will the developer deliver the source files along with the completed training

program? Having the source files allows a company to choose a different developer for updates or modifications (which is especially important if the original developer is no longer in business).
- *Technology*. What technology do they use? What is the history and stability of that technology? Can it be updated and modified in-house? What tools and training are provided for this?
- *Costs*. What are their development costs? Do they provide a range in cost, based on the media, complexity, and number of interactions? If so, can they provide examples of past courses to demonstrate that range? How will payment be distributed (upfront costs and payment schedule throughout the project)? If changes are made in the middle of the development process, what are the additional costs?

Writing a Request for Proposal (RFP)

For a company that is developing e-learning for the first time and therefore has not established a relationship with a developer, a good strategy for sorting the fly-by-night developers from the reputable companies is to solicit an RFP. An RFP is a document that describes a product or service that a company wishes to purchase. It is a public document, distributed to several contractors, which contains enough details about the project to allow for the submission of bids.

Before drafting an RFP, it is necessary to precisely document the product or service that the organization needs. For e-learning development, this means that the majority of the work in the analysis and some of the work in the design phases must be completed first. This level of detail in the RFP will ensure that the developer is capable of meeting budget expectations, along with the desired level of technology and quality. Another planning process that should be completed before writing the RFP is a list of potential developers to which the RFP will be distributed. Recommendations for the list may come from Internet searches, colleagues, trade shows, or professional associations (Rosenberg 2001).

Once these planning steps have been completed, four parts should be included in the RFP (Rosenberg 2001). These are outlined in the following paragraphs.

Part one: Cover letter   The RFP should begin with a cover letter that highlights the key components of the project and the process for proposal submission.

Part two: Standard legal terminology   RFPs should include standard terminology, which is not usually specific to the e-learning project. This section should include information about the organization's proprietary, security, and financial issues. In addition, it should be clear that the RFP is not a contract and is copyrighted by the company. If your organization does not have standardized terminology to describe these items, seek help from the legal or purchasing department.

Part three: Statement of Work (SOW)   The statement of work (SOW) describes the scope of the work required and the timeline for completion. This is the most important component of the RFP, because it conveys the company's expectations for the project. Without a clear SOW, hiring a developer would be a shot in the dark, whereby the lowest bidder would be chosen without any consideration of their ability to meet project requirements.

A SOW requires several pieces of information:

- A short executive summary that succinctly describes the project (limited to one page).
- A description of why the training course is required. This should include a description of the organizational need, without violating competitiveness or confidentiality.
- An overview of the learner population (based on the learner analysis).
- The projected timeline, describing when the project must be completed, and a preliminary schedule.
- The in-house resources that will be committed to the project (personnel, equipment, and so on).
- Examples of broad learning objectives that will be used to determine whether training was successful.
- A description of who will own the intellectual property within the course.
- Expectations of how the course will be managed, updated, and maintained after the project is complete.
- A list of deliverables.

Part four: Proposal submission and selection criteria   This portion of the RFP describes how developers should submit their bids to the company and the criteria by which the winning bid will be selected. This section should include the following information:

- What is expected of potential developers who submit bids (for example, a proposal document of a specific length, face-to-face (F2F) meetings, or a work sample)?
- Specific pricing information, being sure to request the cost for each deliverable or phase of the project. Also, ask for pricing information to be disclosed for services that are not directly needed for this RFP but may be required later.
- The criteria by which proposals will be judged.
- By what delivery method the proposal should be submitted (paper or electronic format), and how many copies are required.
- To whom and how questions should be directed within the aviation company.
- The proposal submission deadline.
- The date when the final decision will be released.

- A contact person within the bidding company.
- Lastly, to avoid companies sending you every project they have completed in the last 20 years, limit the type of information that you will accept. Describe the type of information that will be accepted, such as:
  - biographies of people who will work on the project;
  - references from other companies;
  - the technology and processes that they use (although beware of technology that is proprietary, to avoid unnecessary dependency on a specific company in the future);
  - history of their work with the aviation company (knowing that some departments work in isolation, some developers will attempt to cash in by selling their products to several departments within the same company);
  - the history of the e-learning development company;
  - their client list;
  - types and numbers of work samples;
  - warranty statements.

Development Process

Developing the training program is one of the most time-consuming elements of the entire ID process. Within this process, there are several practical tasks that must be accomplished. These are outlined below.

Interface

The interface that will be used for e-learning must be chosen. The interface can be thought of as the framework within which learning activities are presented to the learner. There is a wide range of authoring tools and LMSs that can be chosen to create the interface. The choice of interface will determine the interactivity and design of the final product. For example, within a large organization, the desire may be to create a company-wide e-learning platform, in which case it would make sense to create a learning portal used in conjunction with an LMS. This allows for easy log-in, high-level organizational functions, and the delivery of many stand-alone courses within an electronic learning library, along with many other functions. However, this approach may be beyond the scope of smaller organizations, such as a fixed-based operator (FBO) flight school, who want only to develop a single two-hour e-learning course within a broader classroom-based curriculum. In this situation, a learning portal and LMS would be overkill, as the organization requires only a single course, which would typically be hosted online.

Learning portal   An easy way for learners to access training must also be created. A good way to do this is to create a learning portal, which is a single website that allows learners to log in and access all of the training materials they require. Within a learning portal, learners can choose the type of content they would like to see. For example, in addition to required training, they can choose to receive company news, internal mail, refresher courses, discussion forums, or performance reports from past courses—or turn these functions off. Using a learning portal removes any confusion about what training each learner should complete and where to access it, as the organization controls the courses that each individual can access. Therefore, when training is required for a specific individual, it appears within that person's learning portal and automatically generates an e-mail reminder. If an LMS is used, the learning portal should be created with it in mind to ensure interoperability (Rosenberg 2001).

Learning Management System (LMS)   Within a learning portal, an LMS provides the back-end functionality of the learning platform. Some of the capabilities that LMSs provide include (Rosenberg 2001):

- Maintaining a company-wide course catalog:
  - allows employees to find and complete training courses on any topics that they are interested in.
- Learner tracking:
  - allows an organization to selectively distribute training materials only to those learners who require training;
  - allows senior management to identify who has been trained and is current on a particular aircraft or system:
    - alerts management when workforce with a particular skill is over- or under-represented.
  - tracks performance and measures time spent in course:
    - provides learner with customized, immediate performance reports.
  - checks the learner's computer hardware and software before starting training for proper configuration.
- Assessments:
  - before training:
    - distribute baseline tests, allowing learners to compare their current level of performance against organizational performance expectations;
    - distribute surveys and questionnaires for selection purposes, identifying personal and professional characteristics and linking them to the learner's success or failure in training.
  - after training:
    - measure learner performance after training to assess how training has improved knowledge, skill, and attitude;

- o alter training plan to address areas where learner requires additional training.
- Compatibility:
  - the LMS must be compatible with the other organizational software platforms, such as the company's e-mail, scheduling, and human resource systems.

There are many LMSs on the market. Because of the number of LMSs and the speed of technological evolution, it is beyond the scope of this work to suggest one in particular. However, the Aviation Industry Computer-Based Training Committee (AICC) is an excellent point of reference for making software decisions (http://www.aicc.org).

Web-based delivery   For smaller organizations that don't wish to invest in a large-scale learning portal and LMS, a good option is to deliver training via a secure website. This is a much more affordable delivery option, although it does not offer the functionality of an LMS. For web-based delivery, an organization would pay an annual fee to register the domain name and a separate fee for web hosting. The domain name is the name of the website, which learners type into their web browser to access the website. Registering the domain name buys the rights to that name, but one must also pay for hosting before the website is accessible. Purchasing web hosting refers to the online 'space' (connectivity, services, and storage) required for the website to be accessible online.

Authoring Tools

No matter whether an e-learning course will be hosted on an LMS within a large airline's training library, or be web-based and used to supplement classroom-based training within a small flight school, it must be built within an authoring system. Although the term *authoring* might suggest that it refers to the writing of content, this is not entirely true. Authoring systems are a type of software that e-learning programmers use to create training programs, using content from the storyboards. If the desire is to create customized e-learning, an authoring tool will be required to integrate the audio, on-screen text, interactions, and quizzes, as well as the structure of adaptive functions. Similar to LMSs, there are many on the market, and each is associated with strengths and weaknesses. Generally speaking, one must pick and choose tools from several different authoring systems to create the best possible e-learning.

Some authoring tools provide templates, allowing individuals with minimal software programming experience to create attractive and functional courseware. This is a good option for medium-sized organizations that wish to develop e-learning in-house. However, templates are limited in their design and in the types of interactions that can be incorporated. Therefore, templates may not be the best option for a large airline that is investing in many e-learning courses (Rosenberg 2001).

Bandwidth

It is also necessary to consider how learners will access the training. High levels of multimedia require a high rate of data transfer, also called bandwidth. For example, if an e-learning program incorporates a lot of video content, there is a lot of data that must be downloaded to the learner's computer before training can begin. Even with a fast Internet connection, this can result in long load times that may discourage the learner. For learners who have slower dial-up Internet connections, transferring large amounts of data could take hours or even days. Horton (2006) suggests that the total file size for each topic (including supporting files) should be limited to a size that can load in less than ten seconds. Before developing training, consider the demographics of learners and the type of equipment they have access to.

Table 10.1   File size limit associated with Internet connection speed

Learner's Internet Connection Speed (kilobit per second [kpbs])	File Size Limit Per Topic (in kilobytes [K])
14.4	10
28.8	20
56	40
128	80
1000 (also referred to as 1 Mbps)	640

Source: Horton 2006.

Production

Once the foundational decisions have been made about how the content will be built, the project manager will oversee the work of the instructional designer, graphic artist, writer, and video and audio producers, to ensure that they finish their components on schedule and deliver them to the software programmer for integration into the training program. The following milestones may be included in the production process.

Rapid prototyping   Rapid prototyping involves taking a small portion of an e-learning program and completely developing it so that key reviewers within a company can get an idea of how the final product will look and act early in the development process. Sometimes, multiple prototypes with key design differences will be developed simultaneously, so that they can be compared to determine which one best fits the company's expectations (Piskurich 2006).

With a rapid prototype, reviewers have the opportunity to try out various design features such as navigation buttons, interactive exercises, graphic design, and games, among others. Early feedback will then be collected and analyzed, and design decisions will be made regarding how these elements should be modified or improved for the final training program.

Small changes, such as moving navigation buttons or changing font size, can impact the program's source code, adding hundreds of hours to programming time. Rapid prototyping allows programmers to ensure that the product they are designing matches the expectations of the organization. This is a very useful strategy, particularly in large-scale projects.

Alpha test Different from a rapid prototype, in which only a small sample of training is used to make early design decisions, an alpha test is a complete and functional version of the training program, which is released to a few key reviewers within an organization. The purpose of the alpha test is to assess functionality of the programming. Reviewers will be asked to take detailed notes of any bugs or problems that are encountered. Typographical errors, incorrect branching, and other small issues associated with how the training was built will be identified in the alpha test. Because of budget and timeline constraints, it is not feasible to make significant design or content changes at this stage. Keep in mind that the purpose of the alpha test is to ensure that the program is functional, not that it is effective for improving performance. This should not be a problem, because at this stage the content, design, and functionality of the course have already been approved. The instructional content is based on the storyboards, which were created in the design phase of ID, and the design and interaction are based on responses to the rapid prototype. However, this fact reiterates the importance of careful planning; the alpha test is not the time to rethink the types of learning activities that were chosen early on. After any problems that were encountered in the alpha test have been resolved, the beta test will be conducted.

Beta test The beta test involves distributing training to actual learners, called beta testers, and tracking their feedback to identify any malfunctions that still exist within the training program. This is a valuable process, as it is the first time that feedback will be received from actual learners. For scheduling purposes, keep in mind that the beta test will take approximately twice as long to complete as the training course alone. The beta testers require this extra time to write out their detailed feedback (Piskurich 2006). Once the beta test is complete, and the software programmer has resolved any bugs that were identified, the e-learning will be ready for implementation.

Conclusion

The development phase of ID requires excellent project management, as a team of people working on various elements must be effectively directed and coordinated to accomplish project goals. Whether training is developed in-house or subcontracted, the quality of training depends heavily on the skill of the development team. Therefore, it is important to find individuals or a company with excellent credentials and experience. Overall, development is an exciting phase in the ID cycle, because it is where the planning and organization is transformed into a functional course. However, it is also important to consider that this phase is often the most time consuming of the ADDIE components.

Practical Summary

- There are two approaches to the development of e-learning: (1) hiring a development team to create training in-house, or (2) hiring an e-learning development company.
- If creating e-learning in-house, several key team members are required for the project:
  - project manager, to manage the timeline, budget, and other team members;
  - subject matter expert (SME), to educate the development team about the culture and rules of thumb of the industry, also to review training at key points;
  - instructional designer, to conduct analysis and design of training and create detailed storyboards;
  - writer, who works with the instructional designer to refine audio script and on-screen text;
  - software programmer, who uses an authoring system to create the training program;
  - graphic artist, to create the artistic elements of the training program;
  - video and audio producers, to record video and audio required for training;
  - reviewers, who are designated instructors and students who review the training.
- If choosing an e-learning development company, be careful to select a reputable company. Consider their:
  - facility and staff;
  - past work;
  - reputation;
  - project management;
  - licensing approach;
  - type of technology;
  - costs.
- A request for proposal (RFP) can be used to help choose the most appropriate and qualified company:
  - RFPs should include the following four elements:
    - a cover letter outlining the project;
    - standard legal terminology outlining company proprietary, security, and financial issues;

- o a statement of work (SOW);
  - o proposal submission and selection criteria.
- Once the development team has been chosen, the actual development process begins. Decisions in this process include:
  - What type of interface will be used? Will the training be accessible through a learning portal and learning management system (LMS) or through web-based delivery?
    - o For large airlines, a learning portal and LMS is probably the best option. For smaller flight schools, web-based delivery is a less expensive yet effective option.
  - Next, an authoring tool will be chosen to create the training program. The authoring tool is the software the developer uses to format the training program and compile text, video, and audio into its final form.
  - Bandwidth—the data transfer rate—should be considered. Incorporation of a lot of multimedia will require a high bandwidth, and learners will need to have a fast Internet connection to use the training.
- There are three significant stages in the e-learning development process:
  - rapid prototyping, in which a small sample of training is fully developed so it can be assessed by decision makers and modified early in the development cycle;
  - alpha testing, the first complete and fully functional version of training, which is distributed to key reviewers to test for functionality and programming errors;
  - beta testing, in which training is reviewed by learner beta-testers, who identify any remaining programming errors.

Chapter 11

Implementation

The value of an idea lies in the using of it.

—Thomas Alva Edison

Overview

The purpose of this chapter is to review important considerations in e-learning implementation, including:

- establishing the information technology (IT) infrastructure;
- creating an e-learning support center;
- internal marketing:
  - educating employees about e-learning;
  - engaging employees by giving them a chance to practice using e-learning;
  - integrating e-learning into training.

Introduction

Similar to the development phase of instructional design (ID), the implementation phase is very practical in nature. If training has been built on a foundation of sound ID principles, the goal of implementation will be simply to deliver the training to learners. However, the process of e-learning implementation should be slightly more involved than sending learners an e-mail with instructions of where to log on. In fact, of all of the Analyze, Design, Develop, Implement, Evaluate (ADDIE) components, implementation is often the most poorly performed (Jonassen, Tessmer and Hannum 1999).

Implementation of e-Learning

The implementation process suggested for aviation e-learning involves several phases, including:

- Ensuring that the information technology (IT) infrastructure is in place:
  - this includes implementing the necessary computer hardware, software, and network.

- The training and scheduling of e-learning support staff who will be available to assist learners who experience technical difficulties.
- An internal marketing campaign to solicit buy-in for e-learning among employees through education, engagement, and eventually integration of e-learning:
  - instructors must be educated about how e-learning works and their role in coaching and supporting learners.

Once these steps have been completed, training delivery is quite straightforward and involves scheduling and granting learners access to training. Once this process has been completed, the evaluation phase will begin. Evaluation, the final component of the ID process, is described in Chapter 12.

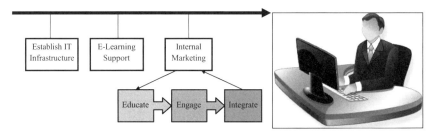

Figure 11.1   The e-learning implementation process

Establish Information Technology (IT) Infrastructure

Up until this point in the e-learning ID process, the focus has been placed on the content of training, because the content is more important than the technology. The technology must enable the accomplishment of the training objectives. Therefore, when choosing technology, organizations must not become seduced by unnecessary and expensive bells and whistles. Because technology evolves rapidly, it is beyond the scope of this book to recommend specific types of technology. It is suggested that organizations reference industry standards (such as those published by the Aviation Industry Computer-based Training Committee (AICC)) and establish a strong relationship with their IT department. In smaller organizations without an IT department, the contracted e-learning developer is often relied upon to fill this role.

Before the e-learning is delivered, several decisions must be made regarding the hardware, software, and computer network that will be used to deliver training. This decision should be made in conjunction with IT or based on recommendations from e-learning development professionals. Once the decision has been made, the chosen hardware and software must be purchased and distributed throughout the organization. This can be accomplished by first buying licenses to the required software and installing it throughout the company's computer network, and then generating a list of required computer hardware and the minimum Internet connection required, and distributing the information to employee learners.

IT decisions should be based on the financial, human, and technological resources available within an organization. Unfortunately, it is common for organizations to invest human and financial resources into the creation of e-learning, and then find out that their computers do not have the software and hardware capacity to support the program. To ensure that an organization has the capacity to deliver e-learning before it is rolled out to learners, it is crucial for the designer to establish a strong relationship with IT professionals. Technological problems can be extremely frustrating for learners and may sour their opinion of an e-learning initiative before training even begins.

e-Learning Support

An e-learning support structure must be established before training is delivered to learners. No matter how well designed and user friendly the e-learning, learners will inevitably encounter problems. When problems are encountered, learners should know which people or tools are available to provide support, and how they can be accessed.

e-Learning support may range in complexity from a single on-duty instructor in a small organization, to a team of IT and training professionals in a large organization. In either case, e-learning support staff must be available through Internet messaging or the telephone to answer questions and troubleshoot problems for learners.

To decrease or eliminate reliance on humans for e-learning support, an electronic performance support system (EPSS) can be developed and integrated into e-learning. An EPSS provides just-in-time, context-specific information, guidance, and/or assistance embedded within training. With an EPSS, learners can be empowered to find the answers to their own questions. The EPSS can be presented as a simple Help button which, when clicked, provides assistance that is specific to the activity the learner is working on. Therefore, assistance is context specific and much more convenient than scrolling through a lengthy text document searching for an answer. EPSSs can also be used to assess each learner's computer to determine if the necessary hardware and software are available. This kind of help is known as just-in-time support, because as soon as a learner logs in to the system, a pop-up message will appear on his or her screen, indicating that he or she needs a newer version of software and providing the Internet link where it can be downloaded. The pop-up message may also include reminders for such things as turning up the speaker volume. In this manner, EPSSs can eliminate problems before a learner even begins training. Although EPSSs do require an investment in planning and programming hours, they may be significantly more cost effective than maintaining a human e-learning support staff.

Internal Marketing

It is important to build an organizational culture of acceptance for e-learning before the training is delivered. An organizational approach should be used to consider all of the departments that will be impacted by e-learning. Of course, the most significant impact of e-learning will be within the training department. However, e-learning will increase the workload of IT professionals, require additional training for schedulers who grant access to e-learning, force managers to access performance records in a new and unfamiliar way, and require interaction from human resources staff. All of the impacted workers must be educated about why e-learning has been chosen, what to expect from it, and how it can help them do their jobs more efficiently.

e-Learning represents a significant change in training delivery, and change often goes hand-in-hand with anxiety. For example, instructors may worry that they are undervalued and are being replaced, or pilots with weak computer skills may fear that they will perform poorly in training. In addition, managers may be concerned that e-learning simply won't be an effective method of training pilots, and that they will eventually will be responsible for scheduling additional F2F courses to make up for e-learning shortcomings. All of these concerns are legitimate and have the potential to damage the organizational culture toward e-learning.

Rather than ignoring employee anxiety, upper management must build a culture of acceptance for e-learning. This can be accomplished through a three-phased internal marketing campaign that educates, engages, and integrates e-learning into employees' day-to-day activities.

Educate

The educate phase teaches employees about the science behind e-learning, the people who were involved in its development, the training objectives being targeted, and how e-learning can help them do their job. This teaching can be accomplished through group meetings, posters, e-mails, or any other medium an organization uses to communicate with employees.

The campaign should adopt a 'What's in it for me' message for each of the employee groups affected by e-learning. For pilots, the campaign may explain the following points:

- e-Learning has been carefully planned:
  - an instructional analysis was performed, which included careful thought and planning to ensure that e-learning targets the knowledge, skill, and attitude required for real-world performance;
  - e-Learning is not replacing all classroom and simulation training. The only content that will be delivered via e-learning is that which does not require human or simulator interaction. This decision was made carefully, in consultation with senior instructors and pilots.

- e-Learning can help you do your job:
  - e-Learning is a tool that can help instructors accomplish training objectives. It is not superior to, nor will it replace, highly qualified flight instructors. In fact, it is likely to make F2F instruction easier. Since learners will already have completed e-learning courses on foundational skills, instructors will be able to focus their attention on the most crucial aspects of instruction. The decision about what content can be feasibly delivered via e-learning was made in consultation with senior instructors within the organization.
- e-Learning improves the efficiency of training:
  - e-Learning can be customized, allowing learners to identify and target areas of weakness. Therefore, time is not wasted practicing skills that have already been mastered. Customization results in a higher level of training efficiency;
  - e-Learning will not take personal time away from family and friends. e-Learning will replace time spent at a training center, and learners will be compensated for time spent in e-learning. If learners encounter legitimate difficulties accessing training, that lost time will also be compensated by the company;
  - e-Learning can provide instant feedback. Unlike a classroom, where learners may not know how well they are doing until an exam, e-learning can assess performance and inform learners of how they are doing continually throughout a training lesson.
- e-Learning is easy to access and use:
  - e-Learning does not require learners to have master computer skills. It is an easy-to-learn system, and supplementary computer training will be provided to any learners who desire it;
  - e-Learning does not require all learners to purchase a top-of-the-line home computer. Computer equipment and quiet space for e-learning will be available within the company;
  - An e-learning support center will be established to provide 24/7 access to help, for when learners encounter technological difficulties.

Train the trainer Another element in the educate phase is teaching the instructional staff to effectively coach students online, interact with e-learning software, and integrate new courses into the broader curriculum. This is referred to as a train-the-trainer (or T-3) session (Piskurich 2006). In a smaller organization, where all instructors have been involved in the ID process since the beginning, T-3 sessions are not necessary. However, in a large organization with a large group of instructors, T-3 sessions are a very important tool that should be used to calibrate instruction.

The purpose of a T-3 session is to inform instructors of the results of the instructional analysis and why e-learning was chosen to supplement the training curriculum. Before a T-3 session, instructors should take the time to complete the e-learning course as students, so that they fully understand the experience. If new to computer-based training (CBT), instructors must also be taught how to interact with the e-learning software.

Once finished training, instructors should meet in a room with one of the course designers to discuss their experience in training. Although such feedback is not the purpose of T-3 sessions, this is an excellent opportunity for the course designer to gather some instructional insights and training ideas for future course revisions. Within this meeting, it is also important to educate instructors about instructional expectations. For example, in asynchronous instruction, a learning activity may require students to read and respond to the forum posts of at least three other learners. In this situation, instructors must be taught to identify the difference between a substantive reply and one that does not include any original thought and is therefore too simplistic. Since this will be a new way of evaluating learners, instructors will require guidance on evaluation techniques. One way of accomplishing this is to create an administration guide. An administration guide provides background course information, such as how the course fits into the broader curriculum and training objectives, along with specific guidance as to how instructors can facilitate and evaluate training most effectively (Piskurich 2006). Although the creation of an administrative guide requires a significant investment of time and resources, it helps standardize the delivery of instruction and provides a clear outline for T-3 sessions.

Overall, T-3 sessions should be conducted in a manner that respects the knowledge and expertise of instructional staff. Beyond teaching instructors how to use e-learning, taking the time to answer questions and discuss the foundational principles behind e-learning may also help with instructor support for e-learning. If instructors genuinely understand and appreciate that e-learning is a helpful tool that may produce better-trained pilots, that knowledge will filter down and make a positive impression on the pilots they teach.

Engage

The second phase of the implementation marketing campaign is engagement. There are two types of engagement: formative and summative. Formative engagement involves asking training managers and senior pilots to become involved in shaping e-learning throughout the entire ID process. This can be accomplished through monthly or bimonthly meetings, in which a group of managers and pilots are updated on the progress of training development and asked for insights or suggestions for improvements. Training managers and senior pilots are more likely to support e-learning (and to vocalize that support to subordinates) if they have been involved in shaping the course. This involvement is also likely to result in training that is better calibrated with real-world needs.

Summative engagement occurs after the final version of e-learning has been completed. The purpose of summative engagement is not to improve the program but to demonstrate training to all employees, to allow them to practice interacting with e-learning, and to ease anxiety about the new method of training delivery. Summative engagement can be accomplished in several ways, such as making lab space available and inviting employees to a discussion-and-practice session; or offering a webinar, which is a live meeting conducted over the Internet. Other possibilities include making a video of a pilot demonstrating e-learning, and e-mailing the video to employees; or conducting one-on-one briefings in front of a computer.

Integrate

Once the educate and engage phases are complete, e-learning must deployed and fully integrated into the training cycle. The method chosen for training delivery (synchronous, asynchronous, or blended learning) will be decided according to the analysis, design, and development decisions made earlier in the ID process. However, the hard work of scheduling and delivering training is accomplished in the integrate phase.

Ultimately, the integration of e-learning should go beyond simple delivery to learners. For example, as crew resource management (CRM) training evolved in the aviation industry, it grew from a topic discussed only in the classroom once a year to a topic that is fully integrated into and tested throughout flight operations. Similar to CRM, e-learning is something that should not be limited to an annual visit to the training center. Rather, e-learning should become a standard tool used to access information, improve skills, and practice new concepts.

Conclusion

The process of implementing e-learning into an organization is very practical in nature. Pitfalls can be avoided by taking certain steps before the e-learning is implemented. These measures include ensuring that all of the necessary technology is in place; creating an e-learning support structure; and calming anxiety through a process of educating, engaging, and finally integrating e-learning into the day-to-day lives of employees. Following these suggestions will help promote the acceptance of e-learning among employees, and avoid the high drop-out rates that are often associated with new e-learning.

Practical Summary

- The implementation phase of instructional design (ID) is very practical, the goal being to deliver training to learners.
- Before e-learning is distributed, an organization must establish the IT infrastructure, develop e-learning support, and complete an internal marketing campaign:

- establishing the IT infrastructure ensures that the hardware, software, and computer network required for training are in place and operational:
  - this is accomplished in conjunction with IT professionals or in consultation with the e-learning developer who built the training course.
- e-Learning support is provided by people or software that assist learners who encounter technological problems:
  - this may take the form of a team of people in a help center, or an electronic performance support system (EPSS) that is built into the e-learning software to deliver just-in-time, context-specific assistance.
- an internal marketing campaign must be launched to foster an organizational culture of acceptance for e-learning. The internal marketing campaign has three phases: educate, engage, and integrate:
  - the educate phase teaches employees about e-learning and calms anxiety associated with the change in training:
    - this includes train-the-trainer (or T-3) sessions, which teach instructors how to use e-learning and how to teach in an electronic environment.
  - the engage phase gives learners the chance to interact with e-learning. There are two types of engagement: formative and summative:
    - formative engagement involves consultations with training managers and senior pilots early in the ID process, to gain their assistance in the creation of effective e-learning;
    - summative engagement occurs once e-learning is complete and allows all employees the chance to practice using the training platform before formal e-learning commences.
  - the final phase is integration, which involves the formal deployment of e-learning into the training cycle.

Chapter 12
Evaluation

However beautiful the strategy, you should occasionally look at the results.
—Sir Winston Churchill

Overview

The purpose of this chapter is to review the evaluation process of e-learning instruction system design (ISD), including:

- the difference between formative and summative evaluation;
- three formative evaluation approaches:
  - connoisseur-based
  - decision-oriented
  - objectives-based.
- the four levels of summative evaluation:
  - reaction
  - learning
  - transfer of training
  - organizational impact.

Introduction

Although evaluation occurs at the end of the analyze, design, develop, implement, evaluate (ADDIE) model, it should be regarded as central to the instructional design (ID) process (as presented in Figure 7.1). Without a proper evaluation, there is no way of knowing whether all of the time spent analyzing, designing, developing, and implementing the training has resulted in improved performance.

In the analysis phase, an important consideration was who was being trained, why they were being trained, and what they needed to know. Similarly, before beginning an evaluation, one must consider who requires evaluation data, what they ultimately want to know, and why certain data must be evaluated (Piskurich 2006). This information will shape the evaluations that are chosen. Just like all other aspects of ID, the evaluation process requires an investment of time and money. Piskurich (2006) suggests that evaluations should only be conducted if someone needs or wants to know the answers that will be produced. Therefore, although this chapter presents four levels of summative evaluation, not all levels are required for every course. If a survey will end up in a locked filing cabinet and never be looked at, it is a waste of resources and should not have been implemented in the first place. Evaluation instruments should be tailored to assess only the aspects of e-learning that are important to the organizational training goals.

Formative and Summative Evaluation

Broadly, two types of evaluation should be included within the ID process: formative and summative. Formative evaluation is used as a tool during training while knowledge, skills, or attitudes are being formed. Formative evaluations provide insight into a course for instructional designers, so that improvements can be made before the course is finalized. Summative evaluations are conducted after e-learning has been delivered to learners, to determine whether or not training was effective. In sum, formative evaluation occurs throughout the analysis, design, development, and implementation phases of the ADDIE model, while summative evaluation is used to assess learning after training is completed, at the end of the ADDIE model.

Formative Evaluation Methods

Flagg (1990) identifies three approaches that can be used to design formative evaluations for e-learning: connoisseur-based, decision-oriented, and objectives-based studies.

Connoisseur-Based Studies

A connoisseur-based study relies on the help of experts within the field to examine and evaluate the strengths and weaknesses of the training program. These are not pilot subject matter experts, but rather experts in specific aspects of e-learning development—such as programmers, training designers, multimedia developers, or training managers. The choice of when to consult each expert depends upon the specific project, with some contributing earlier than others. The goal of this type of evaluation is to assess the accuracy of the e-learning content, objectives, media usage, and ID. A weakness of this approach is that the value of the results will depend upon the expert's expertise, values, and biases. Keep in mind that connoisseur-based studies are meant to analyze the e-learning program and are not good predictors of how students will respond to training.

Decision-Oriented Studies

The purpose of decision-oriented studies is to help instructional designers organize and design the content of training so that it is well suited to the learners. This may occur within the design, development, or implementation phase of ISD. However, the phase at which the decision-oriented study begins will impact its focus. For example:

- Design phase:
  - the focus will be on reviewing the sequence of content, types of media, delivery methods, and organization:
    - as learning cannot be assessed this early, a common formative evaluation approach is to present storyboards to learners and measure how engaged and interested they are in the material.
- Development phase:
  - the focus will be on the tactical decisions required to build the course:
    - an example of how this can be accomplished is to create a paper-based mock-up of the training program. Learners will be asked to respond to the training, and the instructor will physically flip pages to branch learners to different parts of the training program as appropriate:
      - learners will be asked about the appeal, credibility, comprehensibility, and feedback offered within e-learning.
- Implementation phase:
  - the focus will be on managing the program, and on fine-tuning:
    - if it is still financially feasible to make changes, decision-oriented studies are useful;
    - this can be accomplished by presenting learners with a nearly finished version of training and assessing learning and reaction.

Decision-oriented studies collect information about how learners and training managers perceive e-learning. In addition to the examples described, this type of study may use observations, questionnaires, or interviews, or approaches involving control groups or pre- and post-tests. The result of this type of formative evaluation provides the basis for making decisions about the design, development, and/or implementation of e-learning. A drawback of this approach is that the results may identify a problem but offer no guidance on how it may be resolved.

Objectives-Based Studies

The purpose of objectives-based studies is to determine how well learners achieve the training objectives, which were developed within the analysis phase of ISD. Objectives-based studies are conducted near the end of the development phase, perhaps during the alpha or beta test. Typically, a pre- and post-test approach is used to assess how well training objectives have been met. The results provide training managers with the insight to predict how the final version of the training will accomplish its objectives, and quantitatively measures progress. Typically, this type of study is used alongside a decision-oriented study. This pairing of pre- and post-test identifies which objectives were not attained, along with indications of why each objective was not attained.

Keep in mind that at the alpha and beta test stage, major content revisions can be extremely expensive. Therefore, the objectives-based approach may be of limited use for a small e-learning project. However, as a component of an organization-wide e-learning implementation, an objectives-based study of a current project can provide important lessons for future course revisions and improvements. The advantage of this approach is that it estimates whether an e-learning course can achieve its goals and whether revision is cost effective. The weakness is that the data gathered through this approach may identify a problem but fail to determine how the problem can be resolved.

Summative Evaluation Methods

Proper summative evaluation of training should be conducted at four levels, first identified by Kirkpatrick (1998). These levels include learner reaction to training (how satisfied were they with training, did they encounter any difficulties); the amount of learning that took place (did they achieve training objectives); how the learning transfers to the job environment (are they using their new knowledge on the flight deck); and broad organizational results (does the company's safety record improve in the areas being trained, what is the return on investment (ROI)).

Evaluation Type #1: Reaction

The first type of training evaluation assesses learner reaction. A reaction survey is administered after the training is completed, to measure each pilot's level of satisfaction with the e-learning. This is not related to the amount of learning that actually took place, but to each learner's positive or negative feelings toward training. Kirkpatrick (1998) refers to reaction evaluation forms as 'happiness sheets,' as their purpose is to assess how happy learners are with training. Within the aviation industry, some may be of the impression that this type of evaluation is unimportant, that it doesn't matter how happy learners are with training as long as they achieve training objectives. However, this is not necessarily true. There are four important reasons for gathering reactive data:

1. It allows for the identification of weak elements of training, which can be used to revise future courses.
2. It reassures learners that instructors are concerned with the effectiveness of training and willing to make improvements.
3. It presents qualitative data that managers can use to monitor training programs.

4. It presents quantitative data that instructors can use to establish a baseline level, against which future courses can be compared (Kirkpatrick 1998).

Kirkpatrick (1998) presents seven guidelines for developing a reaction survey:

1. Determine what aspects of training you are interested in evaluating:
    - For example, if you are interested in only the e-learning component of a blended learning curriculum, questions should clearly specify that e-learning is being assessed. In addition, questions should separate reactions regarding content from opinions about the delivery platform. Instructors may be interested in reactions to other elements, such as instructional delivery, the schedule, level of motivation before training, effectiveness of supporting materials (such as manuals), and so on.
2. Create a reaction survey:
    - The key to an effective reaction survey is to gather a large amount of information in a manner that takes the learners very little time to complete. Although these surveys are commonly distributed on paper and tabulated by hand, they can be embedded within e-learning and automatically calculated to save time and money.
    - A Likert (1932) scale is commonly used to quantify survey responses by organizing replies within a 5- or 6-point scale (such as that presented in Figure 12.1). Although a 5-point scale is common, it can produce a centralizing tendency, whereby learners choose the middle number (3) without actually reading the questions. Using a 6-point scale avoids this problem, as learners cannot sit on the fence and must choose a number above or below the average.
3. Encourage written responses:
    - The benefit of a Likert scale is that it is quickly completed by learners and easily tabulated. However, it offers no insight into the reason for a particular response, or suggestions for improvement. Therefore, it is important to leave room for learners to write or type in their comments.
4. Ensure that all learners complete forms immediately after training:
    - If forms are not completed immediately after finishing training, learners may forget key issues regarding training, or they may fail to complete the surveys.
5. Encourage honesty:
    - Although many instructors would like to match responses to particular learners, it is more important to get frank and honest feedback that can be used to improve future courses. Therefore, creating surveys that are anonymous or that include an area where students have the *option* of writing their name is suggested.

6. Identify acceptable performance standards and take appropriate action:
   - When all of the numerical responses are added together and then divided by the total number of possible responses (in Figure 12.1 there are 10) an average score is generated. An institution should establish an acceptable performance standard, such as 4.5 out of 6.0. Thus any course that falls below a 4.5 would raise a red flag, alerting a training manager of the poor score. The training manager would then consider changing the course, the instructional context, or (if the ratings continue to score below the standard) the reaction survey itself.
   - Keep in mind that standards are based on results from past courses. For new e-learning courses, it will not be possible to identify a standard until reaction data from several completed courses is available.
7. Communicate results:
   - The final step is to communicate the results of the reaction survey to key representatives within an organization (such as training managers). For a new e-learning initiative, assuming reaction surveys are positive, it may be helpful to integrate survey comments into the internal marketing campaign that is being used to build a culture of acceptance for e-learning among pilots and throughout the organization.

Evaluation Type #2: Learning

Instruction may target one or a combination of the three types of learning: cognitive, psychomotor, and affective. The learning evaluation is meant to identify changes in learner knowledge, skill, or attitude as a result of training. Since the evaluation instruments must be calibrated to specific training objectives, this is a more complicated process to implement than reaction surveys.

Kirkpatrick (1998) describes the following guidelines for conducting learning evaluations:

1. If practical, use a control group:
   - A *control group* is a group of learners who did not receive training. The *experimental group* is the group that completed the training. If, after training, the experimental group have significantly different knowledge, skills, or attitudes than the control group, conclusions can be made regarding the amount and type of learning that resulted from training.
   - There are several important considerations to keep in mind when using a control group. First, both the control group and the experimental group must be similar in key characteristics (such as number of flight hours, captain or first officer rank, or type of aircraft currently flown). From this pool of pilots, individuals must be randomly distributed between experimental and control groups. This procedure helps control for one group having more expertise or motivation than another.

How do you rate the e-learning course?	Terrible	Poor	Fair	Good	Excellent	Exceptional
1. In presenting activities and examples that help you learn	1	2	3	4	5	6
Comments and suggestions:						
2. In presenting material in an interesting and fun manner	1	2	3	4	5	6
Comments and suggestions:						
3. In the ease-of-use of the software	1	2	3	4	5	6
Comments and suggestions:						
4. In the quality and effectiveness of the animated coach character	1	2	3	4	5	6
Comments and suggestions:						
5. In the quality of supporting materials (online manual and help functions)	1	2	3	4	5	6
Comments and suggestions:						
6. In the fairness of the feedback and evaluation	1	2	3	4	5	6
Comments and suggestions:						
7. In the pacing of content (how quickly information is presented to you)	1	2	3	4	5	6
Comments and suggestions:						
8. In the relevance of instruction to your job	1	2	3	4	5	6
Comments and suggestions:						
9. The extent to which you feel the training will help you be a better pilot	1	2	3	4	5	6
Comments and suggestions:						
10. The e-learning course compared to a classroom-based course teaching the same material	1	2	3	4	5	6
Comments and suggestions:						

Instructions:
Please respond frankly and honestly to the following survey. Indicate your response to each question by choosing a number from 1 to 6, where 1 represents 'terrible' and 6 represents 'exceptional'. Please also include any relevant comments or suggestions. Your responses will be used to evaluate this program and your comments and suggestions will help improve the effectiveness of future courses. Including your name is optional; if you would prefer to remain anonymous no one will be able to match your responses to your name.
Name (optional):

What would have improved the course?

Figure 12.1   A reaction survey for e-learning

- This approach is not necessarily feasible within a smaller organization that has a small pool of pilots.
2. Pre- and post-testing:
    - Another approach is to administer a pre-test to learners before training, and a post-test afterwards. Any increases in knowledge or changes in attitude can be attributed to the training program.
    - The post-test will assess the same criteria as the pre-test, but will

use different questions. For example, if the pre-test presents a fill-in-the-blank question about a specific point, the post-test might have a True–False question about the same point. Using different questions in the two tests is important; otherwise, performance gains may be the result of learners remembering the question rather than demonstrating actual learning. A mixture of question styles is recommended for both tests (True/False, multiple choice, short-answer, fill-in-the-blank, and so on).
- Using at least one pre-test question and at least one post-test question for each training objective provides important insight, as e-learning may not be an effective means of accomplishing every training objective. After evaluating the results of several classes of learners on an objective-by-objective basis, it may become apparent that e-learning produces gains in some areas, while others must be delivered in a classroom, full-scale flight simulator, or instrument procedure trainer (IPT).
- Pre- and post-testing can also be used to assess the learning of psychomotor skills. This can be accomplished by asking the student to perform a specific maneuver in an aircraft or simulator, while supervised and graded by an instructor, both before and after training. However, this approach is obviously not feasible for *ab initio* training, where pilots have no skills to begin with.
3. Ensure that *all* learners complete tests *immediately* after training:
- Since both a control group approach and pre- and post-testing rely on statistical analyses, it is very difficult to draw conclusions without all of learners completing tests immediately after training.
4. Review results and make improvements:
- Occasionally, instructors forget that a test of student learning reflects both the work of the student and the effectiveness of the instructor. Therefore, when reviewing the test results, keep in mind that if the majority of learners have difficulty accomplishing a particular training objective, the common denominator is the instruction. Perhaps revising the course content, method of delivery, learning activities, length of training, or another element of the instruction will result in improved learning.

Evaluation Type #3: Transfer of Training

If the learning evaluation and the reaction survey show generally positive results, the training department may consider the course a success. However, an important training question remains: Are pilots capable of using the new knowledge on the job? This is the third type of evaluation, referred to as transfer of training (TOT).

TOT is defined as the real-world application of knowledge, skills, and attitudes learned in training (Machin 2002). Within the aviation domain, TOT evaluation is commonly applied to how flight lessons conducted in a simulator reduce the training required in an aircraft. However, it is also expected that concepts from e-learning and classroom-based instruction will transfer to the cockpit.

Not all transfer is positive. There are actually three types of TOT: (1) positive transfer, (2) negative transfer, and (3) zero transfer. Positive transfer occurs when training helps the learner acquire a skill more quickly than learners who did not receive training. For example, an aviation student who conducts training on a PC-based low-fidelity flight simulator might gain proficiency on a flight skill with less time in the aircraft than a student who did not train in a low-fidelity simulator. Negative transfer occurs when training reduces a learner's ability to gain a new skill. For example, if a low-fidelity simulator is very poorly designed, the student might learn procedures incorrectly or pick up bad habits that require him or her to complete more aircraft training than other students before becoming proficient on a new skill. Lastly, zero transfer refers to training that has no impact on the learner's ability to acquire new skills.

Assessing the TOT associated with e-learning is more complicated than evaluating reaction or learning. Kirkpatrick (1998) suggests several guidelines that can be used to evaluate TOT:

1. Use a control group, if practical:
   - As with assessing learning, a control group methodology is a helpful way of identifying changes between groups of learners. For example, once a group of pilots has completed e-learning, evaluation items relating to the training objectives from the e-learning should be created. These new evaluation items can be assessed during the flight test or proficiency checks of both (1) pilots who received training (experimental group) and (2) pilots who did not receive training (control group). If the experimental group demonstrated better performance on the new evaluation items, it can be concluded that the training positively transferred to real-world operations.
2. Remember, sometimes changes take time:
   - Unlike learning that can be assessed immediately after training is complete, TOT takes time to evaluate. There are three reasons for this:
     i. learners must encounter the opportunity to apply what they have learned;
     ii. new knowledge, skills, and attitudes are applied unpredictably, so pinpointing when to assess them is complicated;
     iii. the pilot may use what he or she has learned, only to decide that they did not like the outcome and choose not to do it again. Therefore, one evaluation may reveal positive transfer, while a later evaluation reveals zero transfer.
   - Evaluating TOT cannot be done effectively in one sitting. This type of evaluation should include multiple assessments over time, that track how the new knowledge is used.

3. Pre- and post-testing
   - A pre- and post-test approach can be used to assess TOT. In this situation, the performance of the pilot would be assessed and recorded before training. This can be accomplished through automated tools, such as the line operations monitoring system (LOMS) often included within flight operations quality assurance (FOQA). LOMS tracks deviations from standard flight profiles, analyzes the results, and presents findings in an understandable format (Speyer 2002). After training is completed, pilot performance is assessed again after a period of time has passed. Comparing the pre- and post-test data allows for conclusions to be made regarding the TOT. This is a good approach when using a control group is not feasible. For example, when providing safety training, it is undesirable to withhold training from a group of pilots, as doing so would place them at greater risk just for the purposes of evaluation. A recent investigation into the effectiveness of e-learning for pilot training utilized pre- and post-testing with LOMS data. Results indicated an increase in aviation safety after e-learning, demonstrating positive TOT (Chuang et al. 2008).
4. Survey others who might observe TOT:
   - Another option is to interview or survey people who are in a position to observe pilots on the job after they have completed training. These people must be familiar with the goals of training and able to recognize whether the concepts are being applied to the real world. Examples of these roles may include first officer, training manager, jump-seat pilot, or flight attendant.
   - Be careful when choosing people for this task, as choosing a subordinate to assess the captain's performance could create tension and unpredictable authority dynamics within the cockpit. Therefore, if this method of evaluation is chosen it must be done thoughtfully, considering the relationships between the learner and the observer.
5. Choose which learners will be assessed:
   - Because of the in-depth nature of TOT evaluation, it might not be feasible to evaluate the transfer of every pilot who completed training. In this situation, a few pilots who completed training should be randomly chosen. Random selection is important, to avoid choosing the favorite or most well-known pilot in the group. The number of learners chosen for assessment will depend on how much of the organization's resources can be dedicated to TOT evaluation.
6. Consider cost and benefits:
   - Compared to the reaction and learning evaluations, TOT evaluation is labor intensive and expensive. Therefore, careful consideration must be given to the benefits of evaluation. For example, if a new e-learning course will be used hundreds of times and scaled up to include pilots throughout a large airline's network, it may be worthwhile to begin by

conducting a full TOT evaluation of the first class of learners. However, as with all methods of evaluation, there must always be a purpose for the evaluation being conducted. If the benefits of this type of evaluation are marginal, perhaps only reaction and learning evaluations should be performed.

Evaluation Type #4: Organizational Impact

The next level of evaluation, assessing organizational impact, is even more complicated than TOT evaluation. An investigation of the impact of training on an organization may focus on factors such as productivity (percentage of on-time arrivals), safety record, rate of turnover, pilot performance, or customer satisfaction. In addition, this type of evaluation might calculate the ROI of training.

Several of the evaluation procedures suggested for earlier evaluation types may be used to assess organizational impact. For example, a control-group approach could be used to compare the on-time arrivals of pilots who have completed training against a group of pilots who have not completed training. Or pre- and post-testing could be applied, in the form of customer satisfaction surveys distributed to passengers before and after a specific group of pilots receive training. However, for an organization, the most significant evaluation is probably the ROI. Assessment of ROI is important, because it provides evidence of whether or not the development and integration of e-learning, which is an expensive endeavor, makes sense financially. ROI is calculated as a ratio of the costs to the benefits of training, as presented in Figure 12.2.

$$ROI\ (\%) = \frac{(Benefits - Costs) \times 100}{Costs}$$

Figure 12.2 Return on investment formula

The ROI formula first determines the total dollar value associated with the benefits of e-learning. Then, the total cost of e-learning development and implementation is subtracted from the benefits. The result is multiplied by 100 and then divided by the cost. The result of this formula is an ROI percentage.

Chuang et al.'s (2008) assessment of the ROI of e-learning identifies the costs and benefits outlined below. The value of the cost and savings for TransAsia Airways, which is a domestic airline in Taiwan, is presented in United States dollars (USD):

- Costs:
  - e-learning expenses:
    - including the learning management system, websites, construction of infrastructure, and course development, among other expenses;
    - 400,000 USD.

- Benefits:
  - flight crew salary:
    - money saved by increasing flying time and reducing training time;
    - 340,000 USD.
  - instructor expenses:
    - savings associated with instructor salaries;
    - 20,000 USD.
  - operating earnings:
    - savings resulting from the ability to schedule additional flights;
    - $840,000 USD.

Therefore, in the TransAsia Airways case, the implementation of e-learning resulted in savings of 800,000 USD. The ROI for TransAsia Airways is calculated as 200 percent, as shown in Figure 12.3. This means that for every dollar invested in the creation of e-learning, 2 dollars were saved. However, this is only for the first year of e-learning implementation. In the years following, savings can be expected to increase as the cost of maintaining e-learning becomes marginal and the 800,000 USD annual savings continue.

$$\frac{[(340{,}000 + 20{,}000 + 840{,}000) - 400{,}000] \times 100}{400{,}000} = 200\,\%$$

Figure 12.3   Return on investment for e-learning in TransAsia Airways

Conclusion

Evaluation is a crucially important element of the ID process. Both formative evaluations (which are conducted during the creation of e-learning) and summative evaluations (which take place after e-learning has been delivered to learners) provide important insights into the effectiveness of training within an organization. The key to evaluation is that, once complete, the results do not lay dormant in a filing cabinet, but rather that they restart the ADDIE process, initiating a continual cycle of improvement. As Sir Winston Churchill once said, success is the ability to go from one failure to another with no loss of enthusiasm.

Practical Summary

- Although evaluation is at the end of the ADDIE model, it is actually a central component of ID.
- Before designing an evaluation, carefully consider who requires the evaluation, why certain data should be collected, and what information is needed.

- There are two types of evaluation:
  1. formative evaluation is used while training is being 'formed,' to improve the course;
  2. summative evaluation is a 'summing up' after training has been delivered to learners, to measure the learning that occurred.
- Three types of formative evaluation are relevant to e-learning in aviation:
  1. connoisseur-based studies, in which experts evaluate the strengths and weaknesses of the e-learning;
  2. decision-oriented studies that involve learners, using their input to make decisions about the organization and design of training;
  3. objectives-based studies, which assess how well learners achieve the training objectives.
- Four types of summative evaluation are relevant to e-learning in aviation:
  1. reaction evaluation, which measures learner satisfaction and feelings about the course;
  2. learning evaluation, which assesses changes in knowledge, skill, or attitude as a result of the course;
  3. transfer of training (TOT) evaluation, which measures the extent to which new knowledge, skills, or attitudes are applied to the pilot's real-world job;
  4. organizational impact evaluation, which assesses broad company-wide impacts of training, such as improved safety record or return on investment (ROI).

References

Ayres, P. and van Gog, T. 2009. State of the art research into Cognitive Load Theory. *Computers in Human Behavior,* 25(2), 253–7.

Bailey, R. 1982. *Human Performance Engineering: A Guide for Systems Designers.* New York: Prentice-Hall.

Baker, D., Prince, C., Shrestha, L., Oser, R. and Salas, E. 1993. Aviation computer games for crew resource management training. *International Journal of Aviation Psychology*, 3(2), 143–56.

Bannert, M. 2002. Managing cognitive load—Recent trends in cognitive load theory. *Learning and Instruction,* 12, 139–46.

Beard, R.L., Salas, E. and Prince, C. 1995. Enhancing transfer of training: Using role-play to foster teamwork in the cockpit. *International Journal of Aviation Psychology,* 5(2), 131–43.

Bell, B.S. and Kozlowski, S.W. 2002. Adaptive guidance: Enhancing self-regulation, knowledge, and performance in technology-based training. *Personnel Psychology,* 55(2), 267–306.

Bernard, R.M., Abrami, P.C., Lou, Y., Borokhovski, E., Wade, A., Wozney, L. et al. 2004. How does distance education compare with classroom instruction? A meta-analysis of the empirical literature. *Review of Educational Research,* 74(3), 379–439.

Bloom, B.S., Engelhart, M.D., Furst, E.J., Hill, W.H. and Krathwohl, D.R. (eds) 1956. *Taxonomy of Educational Objectives: The Classification of Educational Goals. Handbook 1: Cognitive Domain.* New York: David McKay.

Bowers, C.A. and Jentsch, F. 2001. Use of commercial, off-the-shelf, simulations for team research, in *Advances in Human Performance*, edited by E. Salas. Amsterdam, Netherlands: Elsevier Science, 293–317.

Bradshaw, J. (1972). A taxonomy of social need, in *Problems and Progress in Medical Care: Essays on Current Research*, edited by G. Mclachlan. Oxford, Nuffield Provincial Hospital Trust.

Brannick, M.T., Prince, C. and Salas, E. 2005. Can PC-based systems enhance teamwork in the cockpit? *International Journal of Aviation Psychology*, 15(2), 173–87.

Brown, J.S., Collins, A. and Duguid, P. 1989. Situated cognition and the culture of learning. *Educational Researcher,* 18(1), 32–42.

Brown, T. 2005. Towards a model for m-learning in Africa. *International Journal on E-Learning,* 4(3), 299–315.

Burton, J.K. and Merrill, P.F. 1991. Needs assessment: Goals, needs, and priorities, in *Instructional Design: Principles and Applications*, edited by L.J. Briggs et al. 2nd Edition. Englewood Cliffs, NJ: Educational Technology Publications, 17–43.

Cavanaugh, C.S. 2001. The effectiveness of interactive distance education technologies in K-12 learning: A meta-analysis. *International Journal of Educational Telecommunications,* 7(1), 73–88.

Chi, M.T., Glaser, R. and Farr, M. (eds) 1988. *Building Expertise: Cognitive Methods for Training and Performance Improvement.* Hillsdale, NJ: Lawrence Erlbaum Associates.

Chuang, C.-K., Chang, M., Wang, C.-Y., Chung, W.-C. and Chen, G.-D. 2008. Application of e-learning to pilot training at TransAsia Airways in Taiwan. *International Journal on E-Learning,* 7(1), 23–39.

Clark, R.C. 2000. Four architectures of instruction. *Performance Improvement,* 39(10), 31–8.

Clark, R.C. 2003. *Building Expertise: Cognitive Methods for Training and Performance Improvement.* Silver Spring, MD: International Society for Performance Improvement.

Clark, R.C. and Mayer, R.E. 2008. *E-Learning and the Science of Instruction: Proven Guidelines for Consumers and Designers of Multimedia Learning.* San Francisco, CA: Pfeiffer.

Clark, R.C., Nguyen, F. and Sweller, J. 2006. *Efficiency in Learning: Evidence-Based Guidelines to Manage Cognitive Load.* San Francisco, CA: Pfeiffer.

Clark, R.E. 1983. Reconsidering research on learning from media. *Review of Educational Research,* 53(4), 445–60.

Clark, R.E. 1994. Media will never influence learning. *Educational Technology Research and Development,* 42, 21–9.

Collins, A., Brown, J.S. and Holum, A. 2004. Cognitive apprenticeship: Making things visible. *American Educator,* 15(3), 6–11, 38–46.

Collins, A., Brown, J.S. and Newman, S.E. 1989. Cognitive apprenticeship: Teaching the crafts of reading, writing, and mathematics, in *Knowing, Learning, and Instruction: Essays in Honor of Robert Glaser*, edited by L.B. Resnick. Hillsdale, NJ: Lawrence Erlbaum Associates, 253–94.

Cooper, G., Tindall-Ford, S., Chandler, P. and Sweller, J. 2001. Learning by imagining. *Journal of Experimental Psychology: Applied,* 7(1), 68–82.

Cornwall, M.W., Bruscato, M.P. and Barry, S. 1991. Effect of mental practice on isometric muscular strength. *Journal of Orthopedic and Sports Physical Therapy,* 13(5), 231–4.

Costello, D. 2002. *Overview of AICC and SCORM Standards* [Online: NASA E-Learning]. Available at: http://nasapeople.nasa.gov/training/elearning/AICC-SCORM_standards.pdf [accessed: March 26, 2010].

Cowan, N. 2000. The magical number 4 in short-term memory: A reconsideration of mental storage capacity. *Behavioral and Brain Sciences,* 24(1), 87–185.

Davidson-Shivers, G., Tanner, E. and Muilenburg, L. 2000. *Online Discussion: How Do Students Participate?* American Educational Research Association Annual Meeting, New Orleans, LA, April 2000 [ERIC Document Reproduction No. ED443410].

Deci, E.L. and Ryan, R.M. 1985. *Intrinsic Motivation and Self-Determination in Human Behavior.* New York: Plenum Press.

Derouin, R.E., Fritzsche, B.A. and Salas, E. 2005. E-learning in organizations. *Journal of Management,* 31(6), 920–40.

Driskell, J.E., Copper, C. and Moran, A. 1994. Does mental practice enhance performance? *Journal of Applied Psychology,* 79(4), 481–92.

Druckman, D. and Swets, J. 1988. *Enhancing Human Performance.* Washington, DC: National Academy Press.

Duffy, T.M. and Jonassen, D.H. 1992. Constructivism: New implications for instructional technology, in *Constructivism and the Technology of Instruction: A Conversation,* edited by T.M. Duffy and D.H. Jonassen. Hillsdale, NJ: Lawrence Erlbaum Associates, 1–17.

Duncan-Howell, J. and Lee, K.-T. 2007. M-learning: Finding a place for mobile technologies within tertiary educational settings, in *ICT: Providing Choices for Learners and Learning: Proceedings Ascilite Singapore 2007,* 223–32 [Online]. Available at: http://www.ascilite.org.au/conferences/singapore07/procs/duncan-howell.pdf [accessed: March 26, 2010].

Eddy, E.R. and Tannenbaum, S.I. 2003. Transfer in an e-learning context, in *Improving Learning Transfer in Organizations,* edited by E.F. Holton and T.T. Baldwin. San Francisco, CA: Jossey-Bass, 161–94.

Entertainment Software Association. 2009. *2009 Sales, Demographics, and Usage Data: Essential Facts about the Computer and Video Game Industry* [Online: Entertainment Software Association]. Available from: http://www.theesa.com/facts/pdfs/ESA_EF_2009.pdf [accessed March 8, 2010].

Ericsson, K.A. and Charness, N. 1994. Expert performance: Its structure and acquisition. *American Psychologist,* 49(8), 725–47.

Ericsson, K.A., Krampe, R.T. and Tesch-Romer, C. 1993. The role of deliberate practice in the acquisition of expert performance. *Psychological Review,* 100(3), 363–406.

Ericsson, K.A. and Lehmann, A.C. 1996. Expert and exceptional performance: Evidence of maximal adaptation to task constraints. *Annual Review of Psychology,* 47, 273–305.

Eva, K.W., Cunnington, J.P., Reiter, H.I., Keane, D.R. and Norman, G.R. 2004. How can I know what I don't know? Poor self-assessment in a well-defined domain. *Advances in Health Sciences Education,* 9(3), 211–24.

Fadiga, L., Buccino, G., Craighero, L., Fogassi, L., Gallese, V. and Pavesi, G. 1999. Corticospinal excitability is specifically modulated by motor imagery: A magnetic stimulation study. *Neuropsychologia,* 37, 147–58.

Federal Aviation Administration. 2007. *FAA Aerospace Forecasts: Fiscal Years 2007–2020.* Washington, DC: U.S. Department of Transportation.

Feltz, D.L. and Landers, D.M. 1983. The effects of mental practice on motor skill learning and performance: An article. *Journal of Sport Psychology,* 5, 25–57.

FITS. n.d. *Flight Instructor Training Module. Volume 1: FAA/Industry Training Standards* [Online: Federal Aviation Administration]. Available at:

http://www.faa.gov/training_testing/training/fits/training/flight_instructor/media/Volume1.pdf [accessed: March 7, 2010].

Flagg, B.N. 1990. *Formative Evaluation for Educational Technologies.* Hillsdale, NJ: Lawrence Erlbaum Associates.

Flin, R. and Martin, L. 2001. Behavioral markers for crew resource management: A review of current practice. *International Journal of Aviation Psychology,* 11(1), 95–118.

Flin, R., O'Connor, P. and Mearns, K. 2002. Crew resource management: Improving team work in high reliability industries. *Team Performance Management,* 8(3/4), 68–78.

Gaggioli, A., Meneghini, A., Morganti, F., Alcaniz, M. and Riva, G. 2006. A strategy for computer-assisted mental practice in stroke rehabilitation. *Neurorehabilitation and Neural Repair,* 20(4), 503–507.

Gay, K. 1986. *Ergonomics.* Hillsdale, NJ: Enslow.

Georgenson, D.L. 1982. The problem of transfer calls for partnerships. *Training and Development Journal,* 36(10), 75–8.

Goldstein, I.L. and Ford, J.K. 2002. *Training in Organizations: Needs Assessment, Development and Evaluation.* 4th Edition. Belmont, CA: Wadsworth.

Gustafson, K. and Branch, R.M. 1997. *Instructional Design Models.* Syracuse, NY: ERIC.

Hall, C., Buckolz, E. and Fishburne, G.J. 1992. Imagery and the acquisition of motor skills. *Canadian Journal of Sport Sciences,* 17(1), 19–27.

Hall, J. 2003. Assessing learning management systems. *Chief Learning Officer Magazine* [Online, February 13]. Available at: http://www.clomedia.com/contentlanmviewer.asp?a=91&print= [accessed: February 7, 2010].

Heinich, R., Molenda, M. and Russell, J.D. 1992. *Instructional Media and the New Technologies of Instruction.* 4th Edition. New York: Macmillan.

Helmreich, R.L. and Merritt, A.C. 1998. *Culture at Work in Aviation and Medicine: National, Organizational and Professional Influences.* Aldershot, Hants, UK: Ashgate.

Helmreich, R.L., Merritt, A.C. and Wilhelm, J.A. 1999. The evolution of crew resource management training in commercial aviation. *International Journal of Aviation Psychology,* 9(1), 19–32.

Horton, W. 2002. Games that teach: Simple computer games for adults who want to learn, in *The ASTD E-Learning Handbook*, edited by A. Rossett. New York: McGraw-Hill, 139–57.

Horton, W. 2006. *E-Learning by Design.* San Francisco, CA: Pfeiffer.

Hull, D. 1993. *Opening Minds, Opening Doors: The Rebirth of American Education.* Waco, TX: Center for Occupational Research and Development.

Jackson, P.L., Lafleur, M.F., Malouin, F., Richards, C. and Doyon, J. 2001. Potential role of mental practice using motor imagery in neurologic rehabilitation. *Archives of Physical Medical Rehabilitation,* 82(8), 1133–41.

Jensen, R.S. 1995. *Pilot Judgement and Crew Resource Management.* Burlington, VT: Ashgate.

Jentsch, F. and Bowers, C.A. 1998. Evidence for the validity of PC-based simulations in studying aircrew coordination. *International Journal of Aviation Psychology*, 8(3), 243–60.

Jonassen, D. 1993. The trouble with learning environments. *Educational Technology*, 33(1), 35–7.

Jonassen, D. 1999. Designing constructivist learning environments, in *Instructional-Design Theories and Models: A New Paradigm of Instructional Theory*, edited by C.M. Reigeluth. Mahwah, NJ: Lawrence Erlbaum Associates, 215–39.

Jonassen, D.H., Tessmer, M. and Hannum, W.H. 1999. *Task Analysis Methods for Instructional Design*. Mahwah, NJ: Lawrence Erlbaum Associates.

Kalyuga, S., Ayres, P., Chandler, P. and Sweller, J. 2003. The expertise reversal effect. *Educational Psychologist*, 38(1), 23–31.

Kearns, S. In press. Online single-pilot resource management: Assessing the feasibility of computer-based safety training. *International Journal of Aviation Psychology*.

Kirkpatrick, D.L. 1998. *Evaluating Training Programs: The Four Levels*. 3rd Edition. San Francisco, CA: Berrett-Koehler.

Koonce, J.M. and Bramble, W.J. Jr. 1998. Personal computer-based flight training devices. *International Journal of Aviation Psychology*, 8(3), 277–92.

Kraiger, K., Ford, J. K. and Salas, E. 1993. Application of cognitive, skill-based, and affective theories of learning outcomes to new methods of training evaluation. *Journal of Applied Psychology*, 78(2), 311–28.

Kraiger, K. and Jerden, E. 2007. A meta-analytic investigation of learner control: Old findings and new directions, in *Toward a Science of Distributed Learning*, edited by S.M. Fiore and E. Salas. Washington, DC: American Psychological Association, 65–90.

Krathwohl, D.R. 2002. A revision of Bloom's Taxonomy: An overview. *Theory into Practice*, 41(4), 212–18.

Kraus, D., Greenstein, J.S., Gramopadhye, A.K. and Nowaczyk, R.H. 1997. Computer-based team training: The aircraft maintenance environment example. *Proceedings of the Human Factors and Ergonomics Society 41st Annual Meeting*. Volume 2. Santa Monica, CA: Human Factors and Ergonomics Society, 1154–8.

Kruse, K. 2002. *The E-Learning Project Team: Roles and Responsibilities* [Online: E-Learning Guru Articles]. Available at: http://www.e-learningguru.com/articles/art1_4.htm [accessed: March 14, 2009].

Kulik, C.-L. C. and Kulik, J.A. 1991. Effectiveness of computer-based instruction: An updated analysis. *Computers in Human Behavior*, 7, 75–94.

Kulik, J.A. and Kulik, C.-L. 1988. Timing of feedback and verbal learning. *Review of Educational Research*, 58(1), 79–97.

Leahy, W. and Sweller, J. 2004. Cognitive load and the imagination effect. *Applied Cognitive Psychology*, 18(7), 857–75.

Leahy, W. and Sweller, J. 2005. Interactions among the imagination, expertise reversal, and element interactivity effects. *Journal of Experimental Psychology: Applied*, 11(4), 266–76.

Leonardo, M., Fieldman, J., Sadato, N., Campbell, G., Ibanez, V., Cohen, L. et al. 1995. A magnetic resonance functional neuroimaging study of cortical regions associated with motor task execution and motor ideation in humans. *Human Brain Mapping,* 3(2), 83–92.

Lesgold, A., Eggan, G., Katz, S. and Rao, G. 1992. Possibilities for assessment using computer-based apprenticeship environments, in *Cognitive Approaches to Automated Instruction*, edited by J.W. Regian and V.J. Shute. Hillsdale, NJ: Lawrence Erlbaum Associates, 49–81.

Likert, R.A. 1932. A technique for the measurement of attitudes. *Archives of Psychology,* 22, 1–55.

Machin, M.A. 2002. Planning, managing, and optimizing transfer of training, in *Creating, Implementing, and Managing Effective Training and Development*, edited by K. Kraiger. San Francisco, CA: Jossey-Bass, 263–301.

Machtmes, K. and Asher, J.W. 2000. A meta-analysis of the effectiveness of telecourses in distance education. *American Journal of Distance Education,* 14(1), 27–46.

Mager, R.F. 1997. *Making Instruction Work.* Atlanta, GA: CEP Press.

Maring, J.R. 1990. Effects of mental practice on rate of skill acquisition. *Physical Therapy,* 70(3), 165–73.

Martin, B.L. and Briggs, L.J. 1986. *The Affective and Cognitive Domains: Integration for Instruction and Research.* Engelwood Cliffs, NJ: Educational Technology Publications.

Martin, B.L. and Reigeluth, C.M. 1999. Affective education and the affective domain: Implications for instructional-design theories and models, in *Instructional-Design Theories and Models: A New Paradigm of Instructional Theory,* edited by C.M. Reigeluth. Volume II. Mahwah, NJ: Lawrence Erlbaum Associates, 485–509.

McBride, E.R. and Rothstein, A.L. 1979. Mental and physical practice and the learning and retention of open and closed skills. *Perceptual Motor Skills,* 49, 359–65.

McKeogh, A., Lupart, J. and Marini, A. 1996. *Teaching for Transfer: Fostering Generalization in Learning.* Mahwah, NJ: Lawrence Erlbaum Associates.

Merriam, S.B. and Leahy, B. 2005. Learning transfer: A review of the research in adult education and training. *PAACE Journal of Lifelong Learning,* 14, 1–24.

Miller, G.A. 1956. The magical number seven, plus or minus two: Some limits on our capacity to process information. *Psychological Review,* 63, 81–97.

Molenda, M. 2003. *In Search of the Elusive ADDIE Model* [Online: Indiana University]. Available at: http://www.indiana.edu/~molpage/In%20Search%20of%20Elusive%20ADDIE.pdf [accessed: March 15, 2010].

Morrison, G.R., Ross, S.M. and Kemp, J.E. (2004). *Designing Effective Instruction.* 4th Edition. New York: John Wiley & Sons.

NBAA Safety Committee. 2005. *VLJ Training Guidelines for Single Pilot Operations of Very Light Jets and Technically Advanced Aircraft* [Online: National Business Aviation Association]. Available at: http://www.nbaa.org/ops/safety/vlj/ [accessed: July 18, 2008].

Norman, D. 2002. *The Design of Everyday Things.* New York: Doubleday.

Norman, G.R. and Schmidt, H.G. 1992. The psychological basis of problem-based learning: A review of the evidence. *Academic Medicine,* 67(9), 557–65.

Paas, F., Renkl, A. and Sweller, J. 2003. Cognitive load theory and instructional design: Recent developments. *Educational Psychologist,* 38(1), 1–4.

Paivio, A. 1985. Cognitive and motivational functions of imagery in human performance. *Canadian Journal of Applied Sport Sciences,* 10(4), 22S–28S.

Pascual-Leone, A., Dang, N., Cohen, L.G., Brasil-Neto, J.P., Cammarota, A. and Hallett, M. 1995. Modulation of muscle responses evoked by transcranial magnetic stimulation during the acquisition of new fine motor skills. *Journal of Neurophysiology,* 74(3), 1037–45.

Perry, H.M. 1939. The relative efficiency of actual and imaginary practice in five selected tasks. *Archives of Psychology,* 34, 5–75.

Piskurich, G.M. 2006. *Learning ID Fast and Right.* 2nd Edition. San Francisco, CA: Pfeiffer.

Posner, G.J. and Strike, K.A. 1976. A categorization scheme for principles of sequencing content. *Review of Educational Research,* 46(4), 665–90.

Prensky, M. 2001. Digital natives, digital immigrants. *On the Horizon,* 9(5), 1–6.

Raisinghani, M.S., Chowdhury, M., Colquitt, C., Reyes, P.M., Bonakdar, N., Ray, J. et al. 2005. Distance education in the business aviation industry: Issues and opportunities. *Journal of Distance Education Technologies,* 3(1), 20–43.

Reigeluth, C. 1994. The imperative for systemic change, in *Systemic Change in Education,* edited by C. Reigeluth and R. Garfinkle. Englewood Cliffs, NJ: Educational Technology Publications, 3–11.

Reigeluth, C.M. 1999. *Instructional Design Theories and Models: A New Paradigm of Instructional Theory.* Volume II. Mahwah, NJ: Lawrence Erlbaum Associates.

Renkl, A. 1999. Learning mathematics from worked-out examples: Analyzing and fostering self-explanation. *European Journal of Psychology of Education,* 14(4), 477–88.

Resnick, L. 1987. *Education and Learning to Think.* Washington, DC: National Academy Press.

Resnick, L.B. 1989. Introduction, in *Knowing, Learning, and Instruction,* edited by L.B. Resnick. Hillsdale, NJ: Lawrence Erlbaum Associates, 1–25.

Robertson, C.L. 2005. *Development and Transfer of Higher Order Thinking Skills in Pilots.* Ph.D. dissertation, Capella University. Available from: Proquest Digital Dissertations database.

Roschelle, J. 2003. Keynote paper: Unlocking the learning value of wireless mobile devices. *Journal of Computer Assisted Learning,* 19(3), 260–72.

Rosenbaum, D.A., Carlson, R.A. and Gilmore, R.O. 2001. Acquisition of intellectual and perceptual-motor skills. *Annual Review of Psychology,* 52, 453–70.

Rosenberg, M.J. 2001. *E-Learning: Strategies for Delivering Knowledge in the Digital Age.* New York: McGraw-Hill.

Royer, J.M. 1979. Theories of the transfer of learning. *Educational Psychologist,* 14(1), 53–69.
Russell, T.L. 1999. *The No Significant Difference Phenomenon.* Chapel Hill: University of North Carolina, Office of Instructional Telecommunications.
Russell, T.L. 2009. *No Significant Difference Phenomenon* [Online: WCET]. Available at: http://nosignificantdifference.wcet.info/index.asp [accessed March 26, 2010].
Sackett, R.S. 1934. The influence of symbolic rehearsal on the retention of a maze habit. *Journal of General Psychology,* 10, 376–95.
Salas, E., Bowers, C.A. and Rhodenizer, L. 1998. It is not how much you have but how you use it: Toward a rational use of simulation to support aviation training. *International Journal of Aviation Psychology,* 8(3), 197–208.
Salas, E., Burke, C. and Cannon-Bowers, J. 2000. Teamwork: Emerging principles. *International Journal of Management Reviews,* 2(4), 339–56.
Salas, E., Burke, C.S., Bowers, C. and Wilson, K.A. 2001. Team training in the skies: Does crew resource management (CRM) training work? *Human Factors,* 43(4), 641–74.
Salas, E., Kosarzycki, M.P., Burke, C.S., Fiore, S.M. and Stone, D.L. 2002. Emerging themes in distance learning research and practice: Some food for thought. *International Journal of Management Reviews,* 4(2), 135–53.
Salas, E., Rhodenizer, L. and Bowers, C.A. 2000. The design and delivery of crew resource management training: Exploiting available resources. *Human Factors,* 42(3), 490–512.
Salas, E., Wilson, K.A. and Burke, C.S. 2006. Does crew resource management training work? An update, an extension, and some critical needs. *Human Factors,* 48(2), 392–412.
Salden, R.J., Paas, F., Broers, N. and Van Merrienboer, J.G. 2004. Mental effort and performance as determinants for the dynamic selection of learning tasks in air traffic control training. *Instructional Science,* 32(1–2), 153–72.
Seamster, T.L., Redding, R.E. and Kaempf, G.L. 1997. *Applied Cognitive Task Analysis in Aviation.* Aldershot, Hants, UK: Ashgate.
Sitzmann, T., Kraiger, K., Stewart, D. and Wisher, R. 2006. The comparative effectiveness of web-based and classroom instruction: A meta-analysis. *Personnel Psychology,* 59, 623–64.
Smith, P.L. and Ragan, T.J. 2005. *Instructional Design.* 3rd Edition. New York: John Wiley & Sons.
Speyer, J.-J. 2002. *The Flight Operations Monitoring System: A Bundled Approach for Synergistic Safety Management* [Online: American Association for Artificial Intelligence]. Available at: http://www.aaai.org/Papers/HCI/2002/HCI02-002.pdf [accessed: March 15, 2010].
Strait, B. 2006. Welcome to Very Light Jet Magazine. *Very Light Jet Magazine* [Online]. Available from: http://www.verylightjetmagazine.com/editorial.html [accessed: October 8, 2008].

Sweller, J. 1999. *Instructional Design in Technical Areas.* Melbourne, VIC, Australia: ACER Press.

Tallent-Runnels, M.K., Thomas, J.A., Lan, W.Y., Cooper, S., Ahern, T.C., Shaw, S.M. et al. 2006. Teaching courses online: A review of the research. *Review of Educational Research*, 76(1), 93–135.

Tessmer, M. and Harris, D. 1992. *Analysing the Instructional Setting: Environmental Analysis.* Bristol, PA: Taylor & Francis.

Tessmer, M. and Richey, R.C. 1997. The role of context in learning and instructional design. *Educational Technology Research and Development*, 45(2), 85–115.

Thomson NETg. 2002. *Thomson Job Impact Study: The Next Generation of Corporate Learning* [Online]. Available at: http://www.delmarlearning.com/resources/job_impact_study_whitepaper.pdf [accessed: March 26, 2010].

Trollip, S.R. and Jensen, R.S. 1991. *Human Factors for General Aviation.* Englewood, CO: Jeppesen Sanderson.

van Gog, T., Ericsson, K.A., Rikers, R.M. and Paas, F. 2005. Instructional design for advanced learners: Establishing connections between the theoretical frameworks of cognitive load and deliberate practice. *Educational Technology Research and Development*, 53(3), 73–81.

Wagner, E.D. and Wilson, P. 2005. Disconnected. *T+D*, 59(12), 40–43.

Welsh, L.T., Wanberg, C.R., Brown, K.G. and Simmering, M.J. 2003. E-learning: emerging uses, empirical results and future directions. *International Journal of Training and Development*, 7(4), 245–58.

Wenger, E. 1998. *Communities of Practice: Learning as a Social System* [Online]. Available at: http://www.co-i-l.com/coil/knowledge-garden/cop/lss.shtml [accessed: March 26, 2010].

Wickens, C.D., Lee, J.D., Gordon, S.E. and Liu, Y. 2003. *An Introduction to Human Factors Engineering.* New York: Longman.

Wiley, J. and Voss, J. F. 1999. Constructing arguments from multiple sources: Tasks that promote understanding and not just memory for text. *Journal of Educational Psychology*, 91(2), 301–11.

Wohldmann, E.L., Healy, A.F. and Bourne, L.E. Jr. 2007. Pushing the limits of imagination: Mental practice for learning sequences. *Journal of Experimental Psychology*, 33(1), 254–61.

Wong, R.M., Lawson, M.J. and Keeves, J. 2002. The effects of self-explanation training on students' problem-solving in high-school mathematics. *Learning and Instruction*, 12(2), 233–62.

Woolley, N. N. and Jarvis, Y. 2007. Situated cognition and cognitive apprenticeship: A model for teaching and learning clinical skills in a technologically rich and authentic learning environment. *Nurse Education Today*, 27(1), 73–9.

Yue, G. and Cole, K.J. 1992. Strength increases from the motor program comparison of training with maximal voluntary and imagined muscle contractions. *Journal of Neurophysiology*, 67(5), 1114–23.

Zemsky, R. and Massy, W.F. 2004. *Thwarted Innovation: What Happened to E-Learning and Why* [Online: The Learning Alliance]. Available at: http://www.cedma-europe.org/newsletter%20articles/misc/ThwartedInnovation%20(Jun%2004).pdf [accessed: March 26, 2010].

Zhao, Y., Lei, J., Yan, B., Lai, C. and Tan, H.S. 2005. What makes the difference? A practical analysis of research on the effectiveness of distance education. *Teachers College Record,* 107(8), 1836–84.

Index

adaptive advisement 19
adaptive e-learning 18–19
ADDIE model 70–72
advantages of e-learning 6–7
affective domain 101–2
affective learning 32
alpha testing 141
apprenticeships 3–4, 38–40, 118–19
architectures of e-learning design 107, 116–19
asynchronous e-learning 13–14, 26, 111
authoring tools 139
automaticity 34, 56

bandwidth 140
behavioral architecture 117
beta testing 141
blended learning 14, 28, 111–16

CBI (computer-based instruction) 25–6
CBT (computer-based training) 12
CLT (cognitive load theory) 34–5, 61
cognitive apprenticeships 38–40, 118–19
cognitive learning 32
cognitive load theory (CLT) 34–5, 61
cognitive objectives 100–101
collaboration 19–20
communities of practice 19–20
computer-based instruction (CBI) 25–6
computer-based training (CBT) 12
concept-related sequences 109
connoisseur-based studies 154
constructivism 35–6
content sequencing 107, 108–11
contextual analysis 76, 89–93
control groups 158–9
course maps 108, 120–29
courses 120–21
Crew Resource Management training (CRM) 4, 44–52

curriculums 120
customized training 5–6

DE (distance education) 13, 26–7
decision-oriented studies 154–5
declarative knowledge 27
definition of e-learning 13
development companies 134–7
digital divide 15
disadvantages of e-learning 7–8
discovery activities 58
distance education 13, 26–7
dynamic branching 19

effectiveness of e-learning 24–8
electronic readings 57
experimental groups 158
expert performance research 36, 60
expertise 36–7
expertise reversal effect 37
exploratory architecture 117–18
extraneous cognitive load 34
extrinsic motivation 37–8

faded worked examples 57
far-transfer skills 116
feedback 47–8, 52
flight simulation 49
formative evaluation 154–6

GA (general aviation sector) 50
games 58–9
general aviation sector 50
germane cognitive load 34
GMP (guided mental practice) 60, 61–4
goal assessment 75–6, 82–4
graphic artists 133
guided discovery architecture 117
guided mental practice 60, 61–4

history of e-learning 11–12
human memory 33–4

ID (instructional design) 69–72
independent research 58
information technology 146–7
instructional delivery strategy 107, 111–16
instructional design 69–72
instructional designers 132
instructional objectives 102–3
interactions 58
interfaces 137
internal marketing 148–51
Internet 12
intrinsic cognitive load 34
intrinsic motivation 37–8

job aids 58

learner analysis 76, 84–9
learner reaction 156–8
learning activities 121
learning communities 19–20
learning evaluation 158–60
learning management systems 14, 16–17, 138–9
learning portals 138
learning-related sequences 110
lessons 121
LMS (learning management systems) 16–17, 138–9
long-term memory (LTM) 33

m-learning 15–16
memory 33–4
mental practice 60, 61–4
meta-analyses 25–8
military training films 11–12
mobile learning 15–16
modules 121
motivation 37–8
multimedia principles 107, 119–20

near-transfer skills 116
needs assessment 75, 77–80
no-significant-difference debate 24–5

non-technical training 20–21, 44–52
objectives-based studies 155–6
on-the-line learning 115–16
organizational impact 163–4

performance assessment 75, 80–82
performance-based training 6
pilot training 48–50
practice 56–8
pre-training 115
presentations 58
principles of e-learning practice 56–7
procedural knowledge 27
procedural task analysis 96–9
project managers 132
psychological fidelity 49, 59–60
psychomotor learning 32
psychomotor taxonomy 101

rapid e-learning 17
rapid prototyping 140–41
rapid repurposing 17
receptive architecture 116–17
repurposing 17
requests for proposals 135–7
return on investment 163–4
reviewers 133
RFP (requests for proposals) 135–7
ROI (return on investment) 163–4

scenario-based training (SBT) 46
schemas 33–4, 35
self-explanation 62
self-pacing 17–18, 27
shared control 19
simulations 4, 49, 59–61
single-pilot resource management training 50–52
situated learning 119
SME (subject matter experts) 132
soft-skill training 20–21
software programmers 133
SRM (single-pilot resource management training) 50–52
static branching 19
storyboards 108, 122–9
storytelling 57

subject matter experts 132
summative evaluation 156–64
support for e-learning 147
symbolic learning theory 62
synchronous e-learning 13, 26, 111

task analysis 76, 93–9
testing 141
thinking activities 58
TOT *see* transfer of training
trainers 149–50
training activities 121
training centre learning 115
training objectives 76, 99–103
training videos 11–12
TransAsia Airways 23

transfer of training 48, 49–50, 52, 160–63
utilization-related sequences 110

video and audio producers 133
video games 58–9
virtual field trips 57

web-based delivery 139
wireless mobile devices 15–16
WM (working memory) 33
WMDs (wireless mobile devices) 15–16
working memory 33
world-related sequences 109
writers 132